ESTATE PUBL

C000263565

WILTSHIRE

Street maps with index
Administrative Districts
Population Gazetteer
Road Map with index
Postcodes

COUNTY RED BOOKS

This atlas is intended for those requiring street maps of the historical and commercial centres of towns within the county. Each locality is normally presented on one or two pages and although, with many small towns, this space is sufficient to portray the whole urban area, the maps of large towns and cities are for centres only and are not intended to be comprehensive. Such coverage in Super and Local Red Books (see page 2).

Every effort has been made to verify the accuracy of information in this book but the publishers cannot accept responsibility for expense or loss caused by any error or omission. Information that will be of assistance to the user of these maps will be welcomed.

The representation of a road, track or footpath on the maps in this atlas is no evidence of the existence of a right of way.

Street plans prepared and published by ESTATE PUBLICATIONS, Bridewell House, TENTERDEN, KENT, and based upon the ORDNANCE SURVEY mapping with the permission of the Controller of H. M. Stationery Office.

The Publishers acknowledge the co-operation of the local authorities of towns represented in this atlas.

Estate Publications 184 G   ISBN 0 86084 871 X   © Crown Copyright 398713

COUNTY RED BOOK

WILTSHIRE

contains street maps for each town centre

SUPER & LOCAL RED BOOKS

are street atlases with comprehensive local coverage

SALISBURY & WILTON

including: Amesbury, Downton, Mere,
Redlynch, Tisbury etc.

SWINDON

including: Calne, Chippenham,
Marlborough etc.

CONTENTS

COUNTY ADMINISTRATIVE DISTRICTS: pages 4-5

GAZETTEER INDEX TO ROAD MAP: pages 6-7
(with populations)

COUNTY ROAD MAP: pages 8-11

TOWN CENTRE STREET MAPS:

```
┌──────────── LEGEND TO STREET MAPS ────────────┐
│                                                │
│   One-Way Street      →      Post Office    ●  │
│   Pedestrianized      ▨▨▨    Public Convenience  ©  │
│   Car Park            ℗      Place of Worship  +  │
│                                                │
│  Scale of street plans: 4 Inches to 1 mile (unless otherwise stated on the map). │
└────────────────────────────────────────────────┘
```

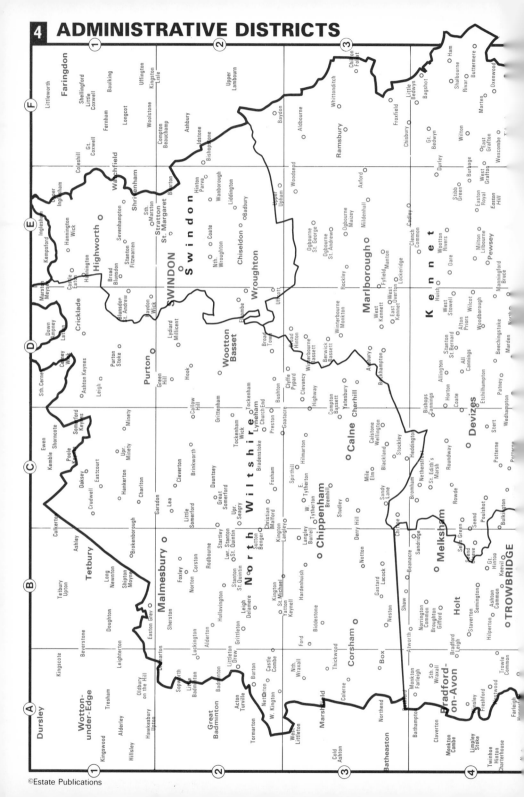

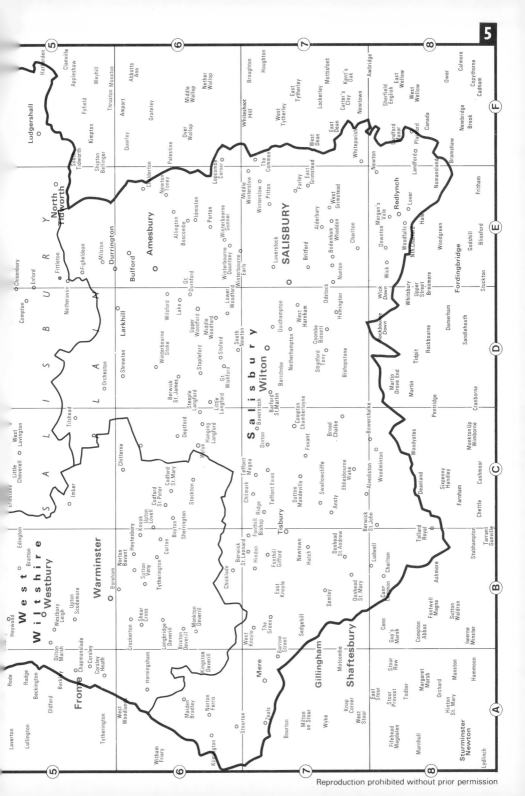

GAZETTEER INDEX TO ROAD MAP
with Populations   County of Wiltshire population **564,471**

Wiltshire Districts:

Kennett	68,526
North Wiltshire	111,974
Salisbury	105,318
Thamesdown	170,850
West Wiltshire	107,803

Aldbourne **1,682**	9 G3
Alderbury **1,859**	11 F9
Alderton	8 B2
All Cannings **555**	9 E5
Allington **469**	8 D5
Allington	11 F8
Alton Priors **230**	9 E5
Alvediston **85**	10 C10
Amesbury **6,656**	11 F7
Ansty **100**	10 C9
Ashton Common	8 B5
Ashton Keynes **1,399**	8 D1
Atworth **943**	8 B4
Avebury **562**	9 E4
Axford	9 F4

Badbury	9 F3
Bagshot	9 G4
Barford St Martin **568**	10 D9
Barrow Street	10 B9
Baverstock	10 D8
Baydon **512**	9 G3
Beanacre	8 C4
Beckhampton	9 E4
Beechingstoke **147**	9 E5
Berwick Bassett **51**	9 E4
Berwick St James **153**	10 D8
Berwick St John **260**	10 C10
Berwick St Leonard **34**	10 C8
Biddestone **466**	8 B3
Bishops Cannings **1032**	8 D5
Bishopstone (Salisbury) **566**	10 D9
Bishopstone (Swindon) **620**	9 G2
Bishopstrow **112**	*
Blackland	8 D4
Blunsdon St Andrew **2,195**	9 E1
Bodenham	11 F9
Boreham	10 C7
Boscombe	11 F8
Bowerchalke **335**	10 D10
Box **3,789**	8 B4
Boyton **162**	10 C8
Bradenstoke	8 D3
Bradford Leigh	8 B5
Bradford-on-Avon **8,815**	8 B5
Bratton **1,193**	10 C6
Braydon **49**	*
Bremhill **984**	8 C4
Brinkworth **1,167**	8 D2
Britford **440**	11 F9
Brixton Deverill **63**	10 B8
Broad Blunsdon	9 E1
Broad Chalke **584**	10 D9
Broad Hinton **629**	9 E3
Broad Town **567**	9 E3
Brokenborough **199**	8 C2
Bromham **1,860**	8 C4
Broughton Gifford **901**	8 B5
Bulford **5,255**	11 F7
Bulkington **268**	8 C5
Burbage **1,434**	9 F5
Burcombe **151**	10 D9
Burton	8 B3
Bushton	8 D3
Buttermere **43**	9 H5

Cadley	9 F4
Callow Hill	8 D2
Calne **13,530**	8 D4

Calstone Wellington	8 D4
Castle Combe **347**	8 B3
Castle Eaton **225**	9 E1
Chapmanslade **588**	10 B7
Charlton (Malmesbury) **428**	8 C2
Charlton (Salisbury)	11 F9
Charlton (Shaftesbury)	10 C10
Charlton (Upavon) **77**	11 E6
Cherhill **712**	8 D4
Cheverell Magna **539**	10 C6
Cheverell Parva **176**	10 D6
Chicklade **71**	10 C8
Chilmark **425**	10 C8
Chilton Foliat **299**	9 G4
Chippenham **25,794**	8 C3
Chirton **409**	10 E6
Chisbury	9 G4
Chiseldon **2,651**	9 F3
Chitterne **289**	10 D7
Chittoe	8 C4
Cholderton **200**	11 F7
Christian Malford **681**	8 C3
Church End	8 D3
Chute (Upr. & Lwr.) **309**	11 G6
Chute Forest **146**	*
Clarendon Park **269**	*
Clench Common	9 F4
Clevancy	8 D3
Cleverton (with Lea) **766**	8 D2
Cliffe Pypard **323**	9 E3
Coate (Devizes)	8 D5
Coate (Swindon)	9 F2
Codford St Mary	10 C8
Codford St Peter	10 C7
Colerne **2,572**	8 B4
Collingbourne Ducis **802**	11 G6
Collingbourne Kingston **454**	11 F6
Compton	11 E6
Compton Bassett **271**	8 D4
Compton Chamberlayne **85**	10 D9
Coombe Bissett **653**	11 E9
Corsham **10,549**	8 B4
Corsley **731**	10 B7
Corsley Heath	10 B7
Corston	8 C2
Corton	10 C7
Covingham **4,128**	*
Cricklade **4,099**	9 E1
Crockerton	10 B7
Crudwell **948**	8 C1

Dauntsey **471**	8 D2
Deptford	10 D8
Derry Hill	8 C4
Devizes **11,250**	8 D5
Dilton Marsh **1,924**	10 B6
Dinton **536**	10 D9
Donhead St Andrew **422**	10 C9
Donhead St Mary **981**	10 C9
Downton **2,784**	11 F10
Durley	9 F5
Durrington **6,926**	11 F7

East Chisenbury	11 E6
Eastcott	10 D6
East Coulston **151**	10 C6
Eastcourt	8 D1
Easterton **591**	10 D6
East Grafton (with West) **603**	9 G5
East Grimstead (with West) **514**	11 F9
East Kennett **100**	9 E4
East Knoyle **645**	10 B9
Easton Grey **70**	8 B2
Easton Royal **260**	9 F5
East Tytherton	8 C3
Ebbesbourne Wake **198**	10 D9

Edington **716**	10 C6
Elcombe	9 E3
Enford **655**	11 E6
Erlestoke **285**	10 C6
Etchilhampton **162**	8 D5
Everleigh **249**	11 F6

Farley (with Pitton) **704**	11 F9
Figheldean **675**	11 E7
Firsdown **611**	*
Fittleton **370**	11 E6
Fonthill Bishop **112**	10 C8
Fonthill Gifford **108**	10 C9
Ford	8 B3
Fosbury	9 G5
Fovant **641**	10 D9
Foxham	8 D3
Foxley	8 C2
Froxfield **356**	9 G4
Fyfield **191**	9 E4

Garsdon	8 C2
Gastard	8 B4
Goatacre	8 D3
Great Bedwyn **1,093**	9 G5
Great Durnford **405**	11 E8
Great Hinton **212**	8 C5
Great Somerford **734**	8 C2
Great Wishford **360**	11 E8
Green Hill	8 D2
Grittenham	8 D2
Grittleton **373**	8 B3

Ham **175**	9 H5
Hanging Langford	10 D8
Hankerton **314**	8 C1
Hannington **228**	9 F1
Hannington Wick	9 F1
Hardenhuish	8 C3
Hatch	10 C9
Hawkeridge	10 B6
Haydon Wick **7,417**	9 E2
Heddington **364**	8 D4
Heytesbury **643**	10 C7
Heywood **459**	10 B6
Highway	8 D3
Highworth **8,668**	9 F1
Hilmarton **798**	8 D3
Hilperton **2,632**	8 B5
Hindon **493**	10 C8
Hinton Parva	9 F2
Holt **1,458**	8 B5
Homington	11 E9
Hook	9 E2
Horningsham **418**	10 B7
Horton	8 D5
Huish **54**	9 E5
Hullavington **1,122**	8 B2

Idmiston **2,177**	11 F8
Imber	10 C7
Inglesham **117**	9 F1

Keevil· **404**	8 C5
Kilmington **282**	10 A8
Kingston Deverill **267**	10 B8
Kington Langley **718**	8 C3
Kington St Michael **695**	8 C3
Knook **61**	10 C7

Lacock **1,068**	8 C4
Lake	11 E8
Landford **1,195**	11 G10
Landford Manor	11 G10
Langley Burrell **412**	8 C3
Larkhill	11 E7
Latton **372**	9 E1
Laverstock **3,029**	11 F9

6

Place	Pop.	Grid
Lea (with Cleverton)	**766**	8 C2
Leigh	**283**	8 D1
Leigh Delamere		8 B3
Liddington	**343**	9 F2
Limpley Stoke	**627**	9 A5
Little Bedwyn	**286**	9 G4
Little Langford		10 D8
Little Somerford	**416**	8 C2
Littleton Drew		8 B3
Littleton Pannell		10 D6
Lockeridge		9 E4
Longbridge Deverill	**851**	10 B7
Lopcombe Corner		11 F8
Lover		11 F10
Lower Stanton St Quintin		8 C3
Lower Woodford		11 E8
Luckington	**508**	8 B2
Ludgershall	**3,379**	11 G6
Ludwell		10 C10
Lydiard Millicent	**1,203**	9 E2
Lydiard Tregoze	**382**	*
Lyneham	**4,747**	8 D3
Maiden Bradley	**328**	10 A8
Malmesbury	**3,999**	8 C2
Manningford Bohune		9 E5
Manningford Bruce		9 E5
Manton		9 F4
Marden	**155**	9 E5
Market Lavington	**1,858**	10 D6
Marlborough	**6,788**	9 E4
Marston	**142**	8 C5
Marston Meysey	**209**	9 E1
Marten		9 G5
Melksham	**12,788**	8 C5
Mere	**2,257**	10 B8
Middle Winterslow		11 F8
Middle Woodford		11 E8
Mildenhall	**472**	9 F4
Mile Elm		8 D4
Milston	**126**	11 F7
Milton Lilbourne	**484**	9 F5
Minety	**1,325**	8 D1
Monkton Deverill		10 B8
Monkton Farleigh	**478**	8 B4
Morgan's Vale		11 F10
Neston		8 B4
Netheravon	**1,146**	11 E6
Netherhampton	**158**	11 E9
Netherstreet		8 D4
Nettleton	**569**	8 B3
Newton Toney	**373**	11 F8
Newtown		10 C9
Normansland		11 F10
Norrington Common		8 B5
North Bradley	**1,770**	10 B6
North Newnton	**414**	9 E5
North Tidworth	**5,813**	11 F6
North Wraxall	**360**	8 B3
North Wroughton		9 F2
Norton	**114**	8 B2
Norton Bavant	**109**	10 C7
Norton Ferris		10 A8
Notton		8 C4
Nunton		11 E9
Oaksey	**443**	8 D1
Oare		9 F5
Odstock	**548**	11 E9
Ogbourne Maizey		9 F4
Ogbourne St Andrew	**262**	9 F4
Ogbourne St George	**399**	9 F3
Orcheston	**282**	10 D7
Oxenwood		9 G5
Patney	**149**	8 D5
Pewsey	**2,831** '	9 F5
Pitton (with Farley)	**704**	11 F9
Plaitford		11 G10
Porton		11 F8
Potterne	**1,590**	8 D5
Potterne Wick		8 D5
Poulshot	**352**	8 C5
Preshute	**160**	*
Preston		8 D3
Purton	**3,879**	9 E2
Purton Stoke		9 E1
Quidhampton	**363**	11 E9
Ramsbury	**1,877**	9 G4
Redlynch	**3,158**	11 F10
Ridge		10 C8
Rivar		9 G5
Rockley		9 E4
Rodbourne		8 C2
Roundway	**1,633**	8 D5
Rowde	**1,294**	8 C5
Rushall	**114**	10 E6
St Edith's Marsh		8 D5
Salisbury	**36,890**	11 F9
Sandridge		8 C4
Sandy Lane		8 C4
Savernake	**194**	*
Sedgehill & Semley	**584**	10 B9
Seend	**1,089**	8 C5
Seend Cleeve		8 C5
Sells Green		8 C5
Semington	**803**	8 C5
Sevenhampton		9 F1
Shalbourne	**550**	9 G5
Shaw		8 B4
Sherrington	**70**	10 C8
Shear Cross		10 B7
Sherston	**1,372**	8 B2
Shrewton	**1,780**	10 D7
Sopworth	**81**	8 B2
South Marston	**703**	9 F2
South Newton	**696**	11 E8
Southwick	**1,971**	10 B6
South Wraxall	**397**	8 B5
Spirthill		8 D3
Stanton Fitzwarren	**211**	9 F1
Stanton St Bernard	**141**	9 E5
Stanton St Quintin	**747**	8 C3
Stapleford	**249**	11 E8
Startley		8 C2
Staverton	**306**	8 B5
Steeple Ashton	**955**	8 C5
Steeple Langford	**517**	10 D8
Stert	**167**	8 D5
Stibb Green		9 F5
Stockley		8 D4
Stockton	**192**	10 C8
Stoford		11 E8
Stourton	**201**	10 A8
Stratford Toney	**70**	11 E9
Stratton St Margaret	**13,383**	9 F2
Studley		8 C4
Sutton Benger	**904**	8 C3
Sutton Mandeville	**215**	10 D9
Sutton Veny	**585**	10 C7
Swallowcliffe	**184**	10 C9
Swindon	**127,348**	9 E2
Teffont Evias		10 D9
Teffont Magna	**216**	10 D8
The Common		11 F8
The Green		10 B9
Thickwood		8 B4
Tidcombe (with Fosbury)	**105**	9 G5
Tilshead	**343**	10 D7
Tisbury	**1,836**	10 C9
Tockenham	**221**	8 D3
Tockenham Wick		8 D3
Tollard Royal	**106**	10 C10
Trowbridge	**25,279**	8 B5
Trowle Common		8 B5
Tytherington		10 C7
Uffcott		9 E3
Upavon	**1,241**	11 E6
Upper Inglesham		9 F1
Upper Minety		8 D1
Upper Seagry	**270**	8 C3
Upper Upham		9 F3
Upper Woodford	**447**	11 E8
Upton Lovell	**144**	10 C7
Upton Scudamore	**250**	10 B7
Urchfont	**977**	8 D5
Wanborough	**1,478**	9 F2
Warminster	**16,267**	10 B7
Wedhampton		8 D5
West Ashton	**387**	10 B6
Westbury.	**9,939**	10 B6
Westbury Leigh		10 B6
West Dean	220	11 G9
West Grafton (with East)	**603**	9 F5
West Grimstead (with East)	**514**	11 F9
West Harnham		11 E9
West Kennett		9 E4
West Kington		8 B3
West Knoyle	**139**	10 B8
West Lavington	**1,076**	10 D6
West Overton	**629**	9 E4
West Stowell		9 E5
West Tisbury	**577**	*
West Tytherton		8 C3
Westwood	**1,195**	8 B5
Wexcombe		9 G5
Whaddon		11 F9
Whiteparish	**1,313**	11 F10
Whittonditch		9 G4
Wick		11 F10
Wilcot	**549**	9 E5
Wilsford (Amesbury)	**120**	11 E8
Wilsford (Upavon)		10 E6
Wilton (Marlborough)		9 G5
Wilton (Salisbury)	**3,717**	11 E9
Wingfield	**385**	10 B6
Winsley	**1,834**	8 B5
Winterbourne Bassett	**123**	9 E3
Winterbourne Dauntsey		11 F8
Winterbourne Earls	**1,266**	11 F8
Winterbourne Gunner		11 F8
Winterbourne Monkton	**161**	9 E4
Winterbourne Stoke	**193**	11 F7
Winterslow	**1,836**	11 F8
Woodborough	**264**	9 E5
Woodfalls		11 F10
Woodminton		10 D10
Woodsend		9 F3
Wootton Bassett	**10,524**	9 E2
Wootton Rivers	**271**	9 F5
Worton	**601**	8 C5
Wroughton.	**7,111**	9 E3
Wylye	**409**	10 D8
Yatesbury		8 D4
Yatton Keynell	**656**	8 B3
Zeals	**636**	10 A9

Population figures are based upon the 1991 census and relate to the local authority or parish as constituted at that date. Places with no popoulation figure form part of a larger local authority area or parish. Boundaries of local authority areas are shown on page 4.

Thamesdown Borough Council has now become a Unitary Authority.

Population figures in bold type.

*Places not included on map due to limitation of space.

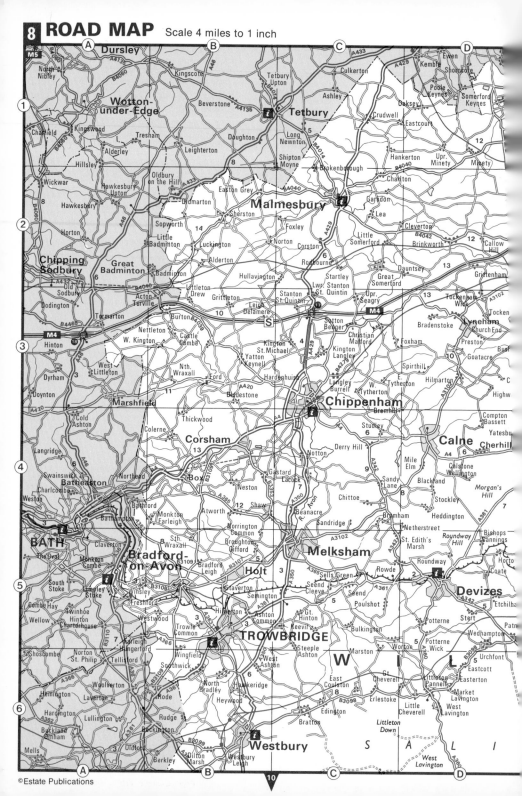

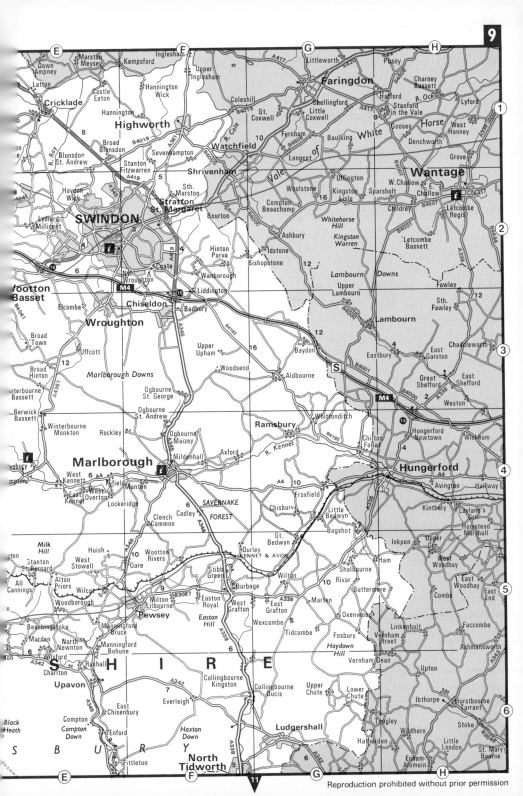

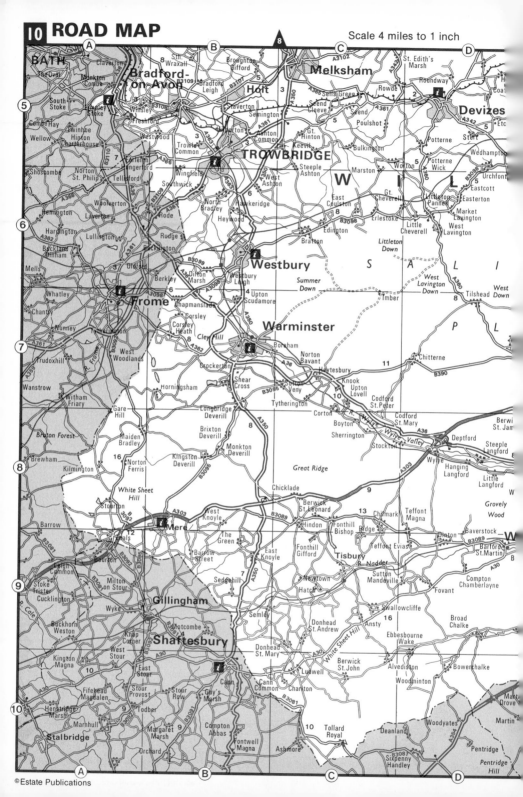

Scale 4 miles to 1 inch

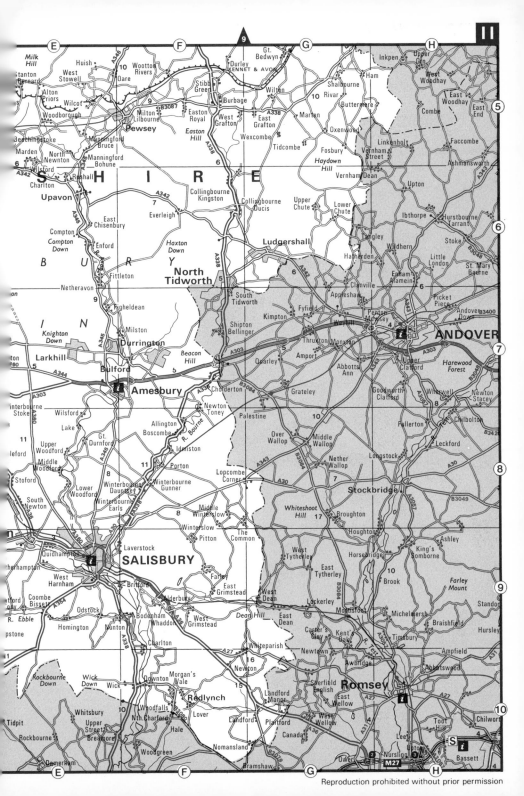

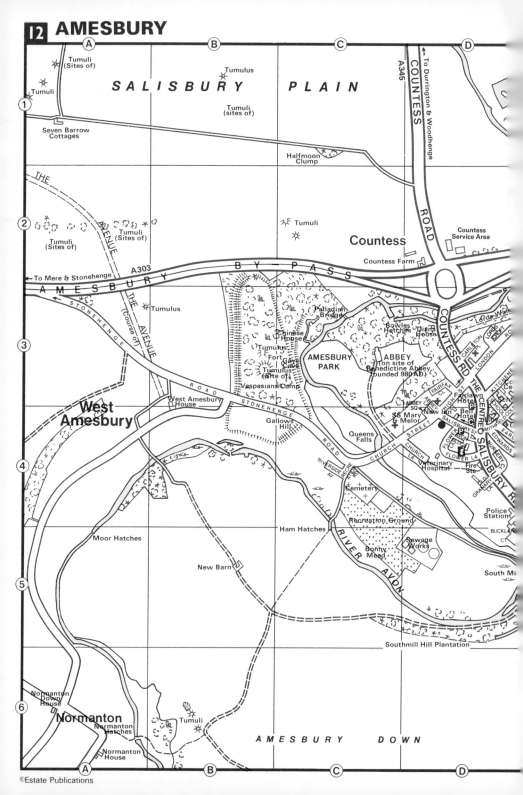

SALISBURY PLAIN

Tumuli (Sites of)

Tumuli

Tumulus

Tumuli (sites of)

Seven Barrow Cottages

A345 COUNTESS ROAD

↑ To Durrington & Woodhenge

Halfmoon Clump

THE AVENUE

Tumuli

Tumuli (Sites of)

Tumuli (Sites of)

Tumuli

Countess

Countess Service Area

A303 AMESBURY BY-PASS

← To Mere & Stonehenge

Countess Farm

THE AVENUE (Course of)

STONEHENGE

Tumulus

Palladian Bridge

Bowles Hatches

Diana House

Countess Farm

Lords Walk

CARLTON PL.

Chinese House

Tumulus Fort Cave Tumulus (Site of)

AMESBURY PARK

ABBEY (on site of Benedictine Abbey founded 980 AD)

FAIRLAWN

FAIRFAX CT.

Fairlawn Hotel

Bell Hotel

London Rd

KITCHEN

STONEHENGE ROAD

West Amesbury House

Vespasians Camp

West Amesbury

Gallows Hill

SS. Mary & Melor

New Inn

SALISBURY ST.

HIGH ST.

FLOWER LA.

NURSERY

SMITH

EARL

West Amesbury

Queens Falls

CHURCH ST.

CHURCH LA.

FLOWER LA.

SALISBURY RD

EDWARDS

Veterinary Hospital

Fire Sta.

RIVERSIDE AV.

RECRE.

Cemetery

GRAHAM

Moor Hatches

Ham Hatches

Recreation Ground

Bonny Mead

Sewage Works

Police Station

BUCKLAN CT.

RIVER AVON

South Mi

New Barn

Southmill Hill Plantation

Normanton Down House

Normanton

Normanton Hatches

Tumuli

AMESBURY DOWN

Normanton House

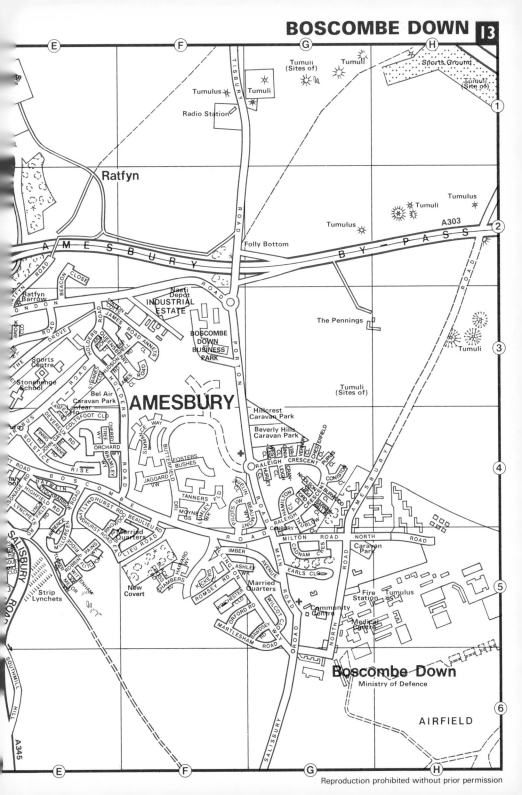

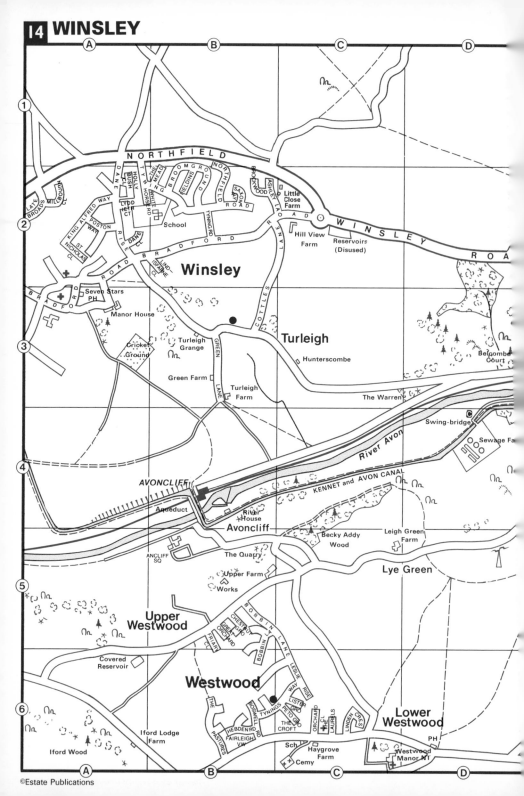

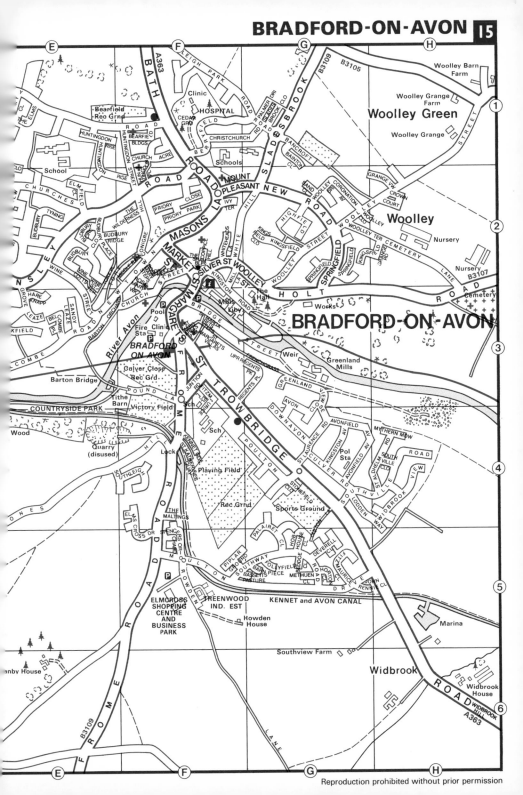

BRADFORD-ON-AVON | 15

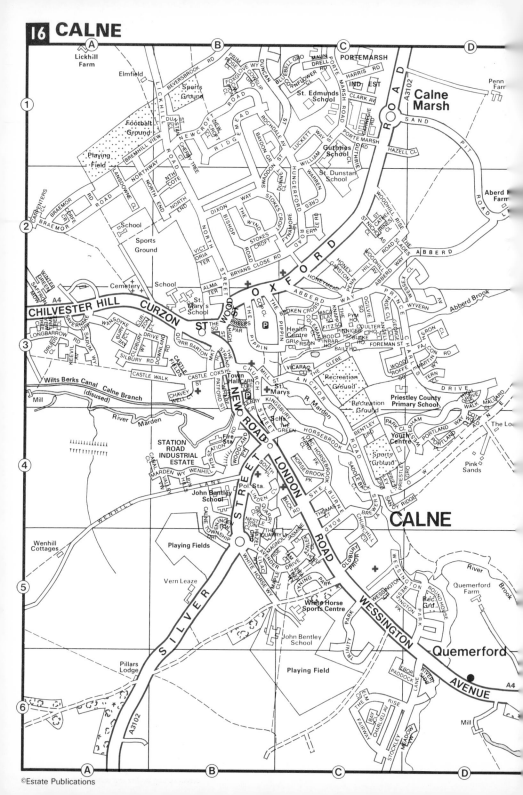

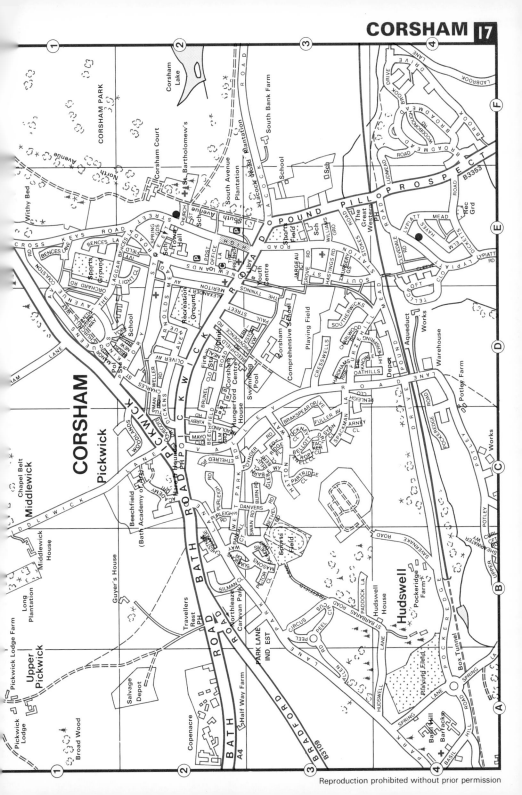

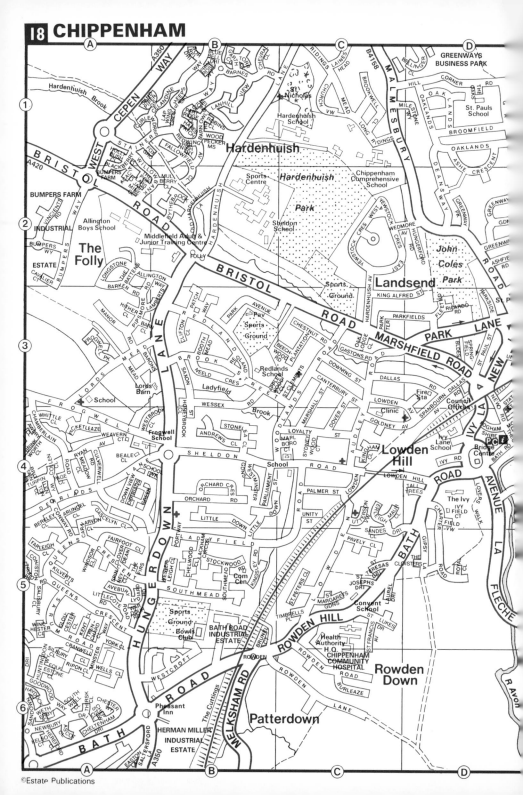

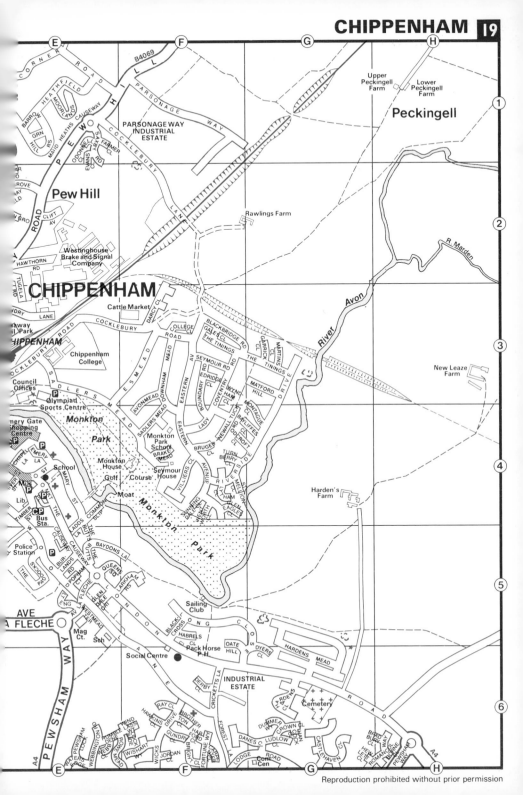

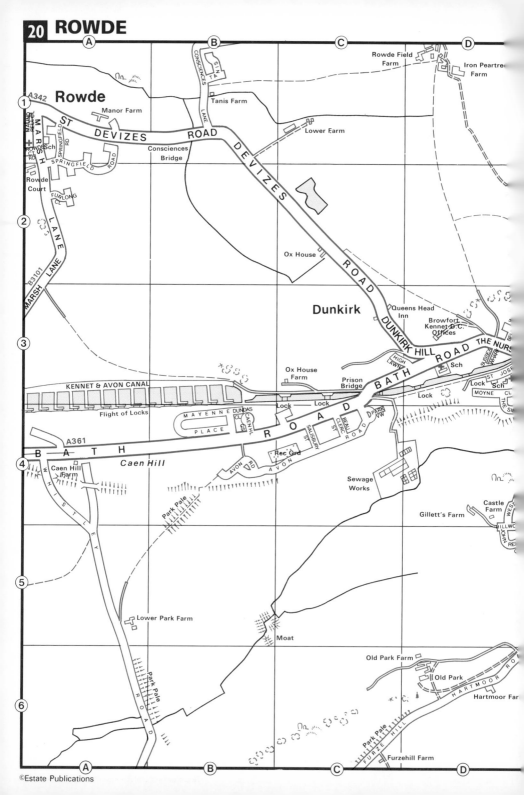

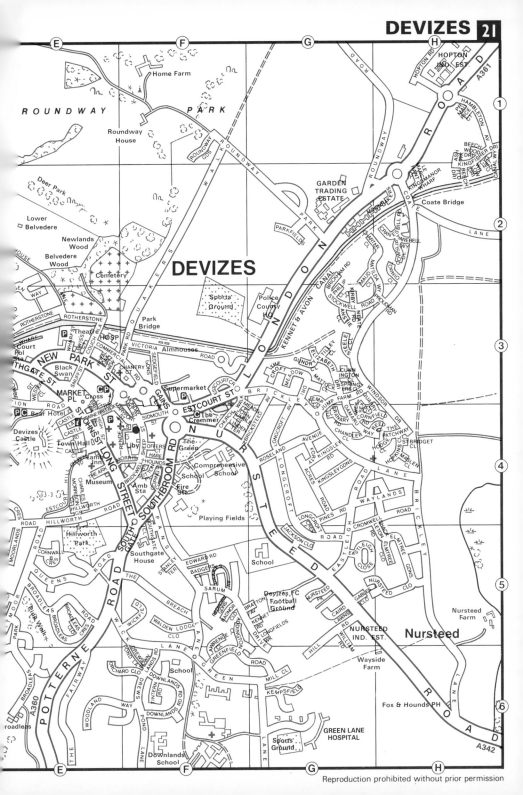

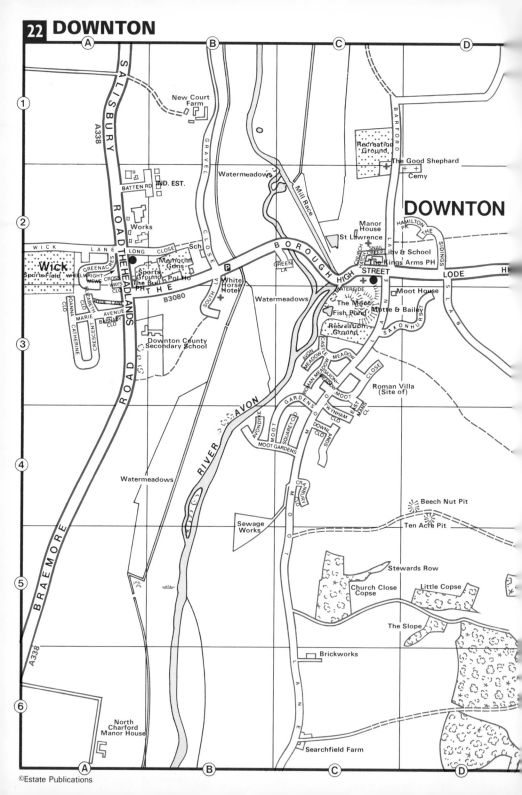

DOWNTON

Wick

New Court Farm

SALISBURY ROAD A338

THE HEADLANDS

BATTEN RD IND. EST.

Works

WICK

Sports Field

Wheelwright Mews

Greenacres

Cross Ways Clo

Elizabeth Clo

Rowde Lane

Joanna Clo

Catherine Clo

Marie Clo

Crescent

Barnaby Clo

Avenue

Memorial Gdns

Sports Ground

The Bull PH

Pol Ho

Long Close

Sch

School La

South La

B3080

White Horse Hotel

Downton County Secondary School

GRAVEL

CLOSE

Watermeadows

Mill Race

GREEN LA

BOROUGH

HIGH STREET

Manor House

St Lawrence

CHURCH HATCHER

SNAIL CREEP

Recreation Ground

The Good Shephard Cemy

Lib y & School

The Kings Arms PH

HAMILTON PK

THE SIDINGS

LODE HI

SLAB

BARFORD

Waterside

The Moot

Fish Pond

Motte & Bailey

Moot House

SAXON HU

Recreation Ground

AVON MEADOW

CASTLE MEADOW

ROMAN MEADOW

MONK MOOT

CLOSE

Roman Villa (Site of)

TWYNHAM CLO

EAST MANS CLO

AVON CLO

MOOT GARDENS

QUARLEY CLO

DOWNL CLOSE

MOOT GARDENS

AVON CLO

M

CRANBURY

Watermeadows

RIVER AVON

BRAEMORE

A338

Watermeadows

Sewage Works

Beech Nut Pit

Ten Acre Pit

Stewards Row

Church Close Copse

Little Copse

The Slope

Brickworks

LANE

North Charford Manor House

Searchfield Farm

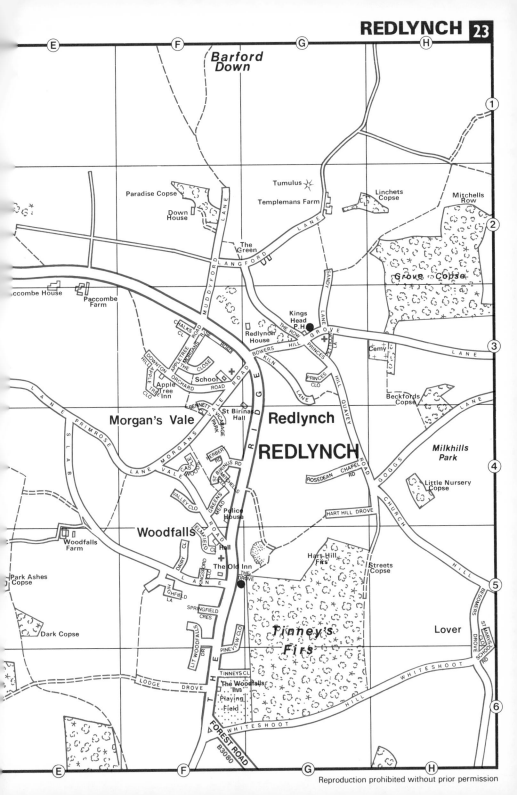

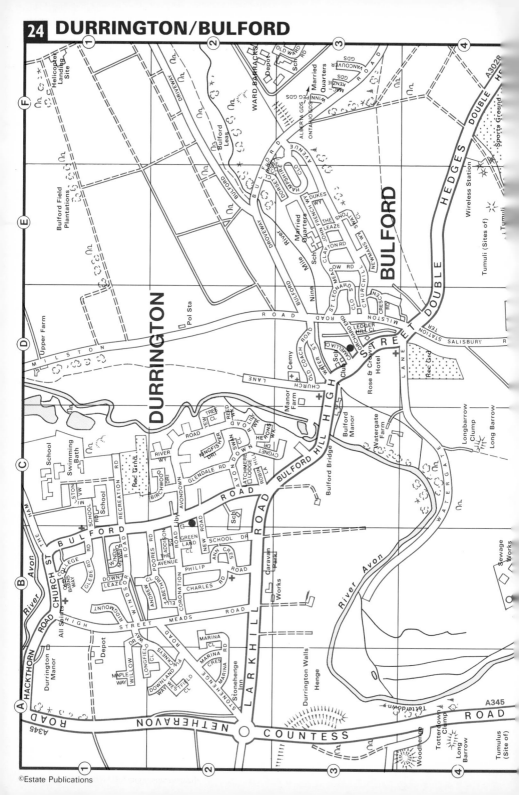

BULFORD

DURRINGTON

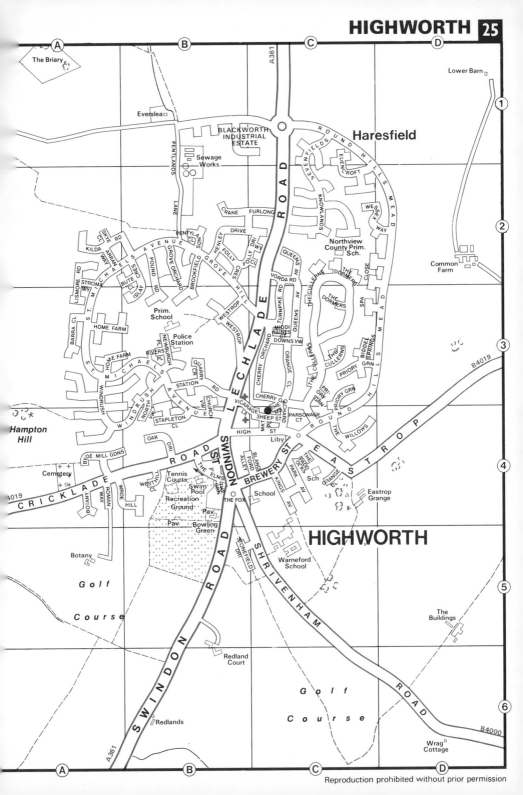

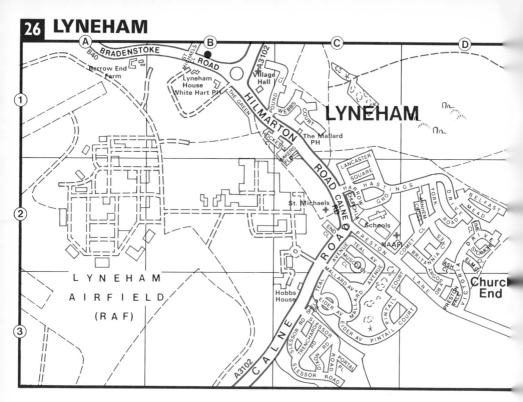

POTTERNE

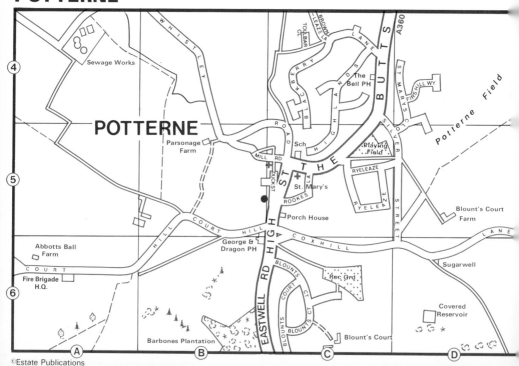

©Estate Publications

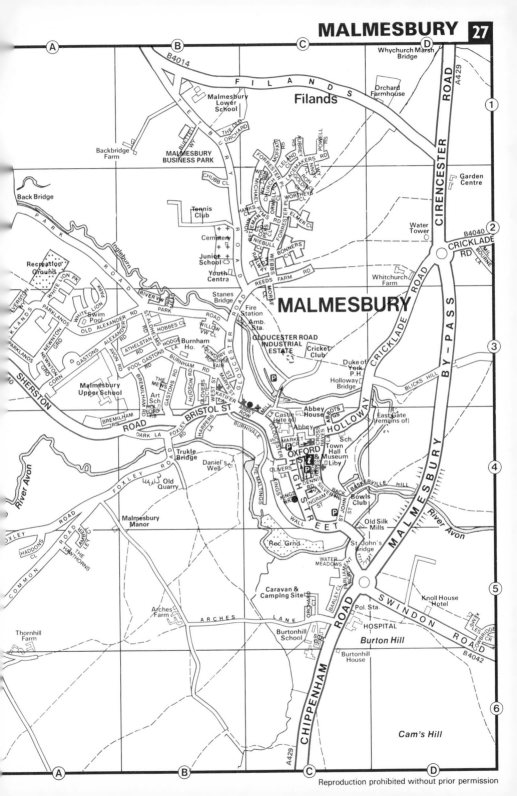

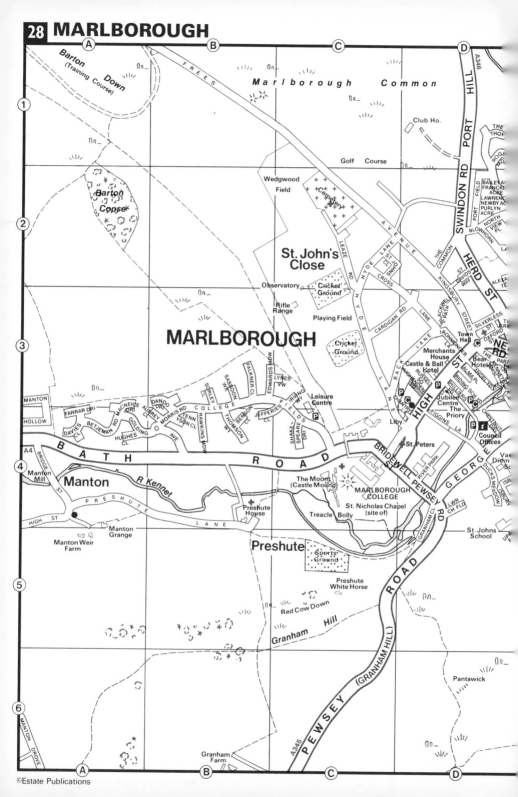

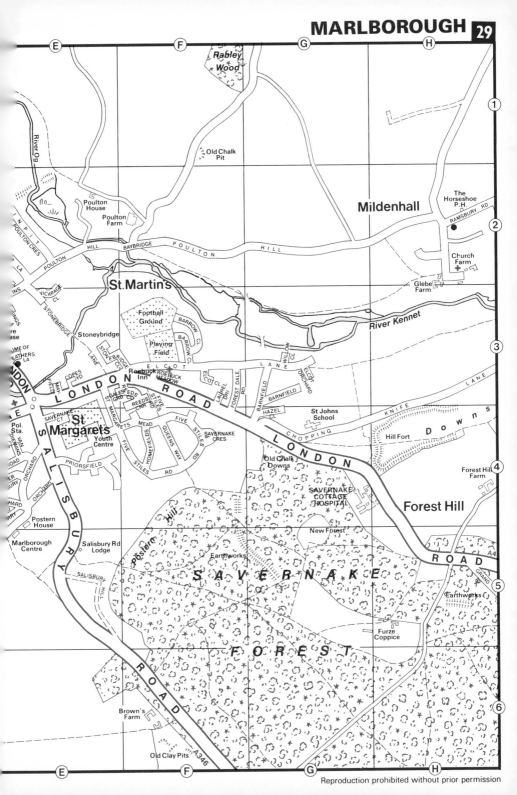

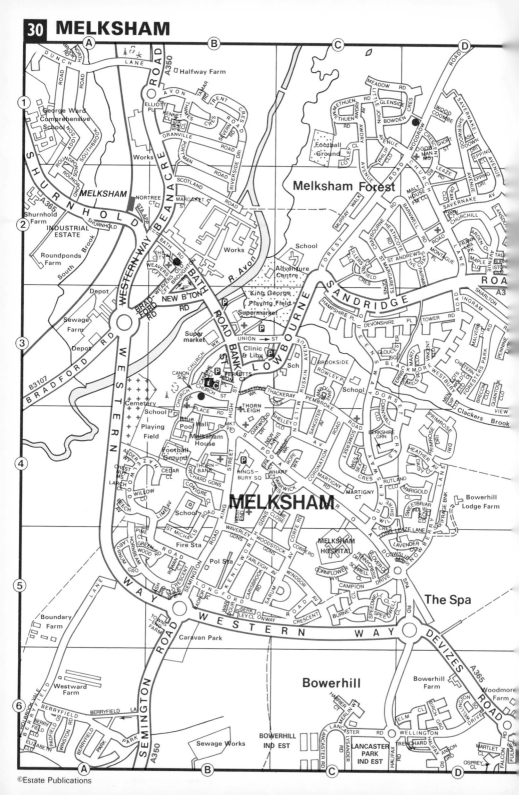

30 MELKSHAM

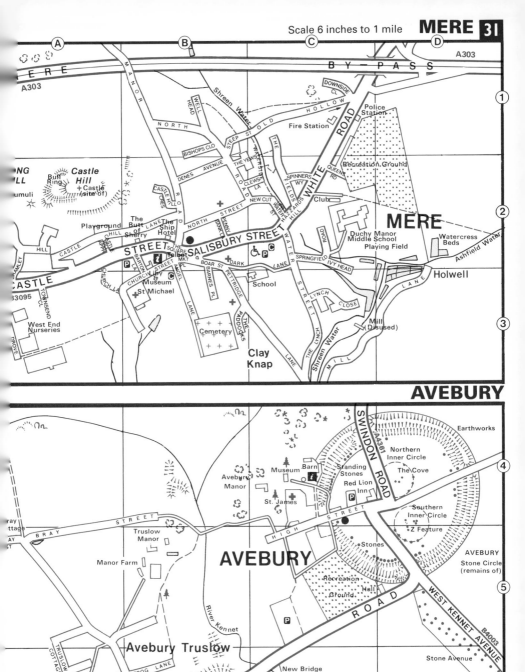

MERE

A303

MERE BY-PASS

A303

DOWNSIDE CL

Police Station

Fire Station

Recreation Ground

WELL HEAD

Shreen Water

NORTH

ST OLD

HOLLOW

WHITE ROAD

QUEENS RD

BISHOPS CLO

STEP ST

THE VENS

CLEWS

NEW CUT

DENES AVENUE

CASTLE CRES

THE

WATER

SPINNERS WY

HAZZARDS

HILLS

FIELDS

Club

Duchy Manor Middle School Playing Field

MERE

Watercress Beds

Ashfield Water

ING HILL

Tumuli

Butt Ring

Castle Hill

+ Castle (site of)

Playground

The Sherry

CASTLE LANE

The Ship Hotel

CHILL LANE

HILL

CASTLE

NORTH STREET

FERN BANK

SQUARE

STREET

BARTON

CHURCH LANE

STREET **SALISBURY STREET**

BOAR ST

Talbot

MKT

ST PETRIDGE

DARK

WATER STREET

LANE

SPRINGFIELD

IVY HEAD

Holwell

CASTLE

B3095

TOWNSEND

St Michael

Museum

BARNES PL

School

THE

PADDOCKS

Cemetery

Clay Knap

THE LYNCH LANE

SHREEN WATER

MILL

LYNCH CLOSE

Mill (Disused)

West End Nurseries

DROVE

AVEBURY

SWINDON ROAD

A4361

Earthworks

Northern Inner Circle

The Cove

Museum

Barn

Standing Stones

Red Lion Inn

Southern Inner Circle

Z Feature

AVEBURY

Avebury Manor

St. James

HIGH STREET

Stones

AVEBURY Stone Circle (remains of)

STREET

BRAY

Truslow Manor

Manor Farm

Recreation Ground

Hall

WEST KENNET AVENUE

B4003

Bray Cottage

River Kennet

Stone Avenue

Avebury Truslow

TRUSLOW COTTAGES

SOUTH STREET

FROG LANE

New Bridge

BECKHAMPTON

NASH ROAD

A4361

WADEN HILL

Tumulus

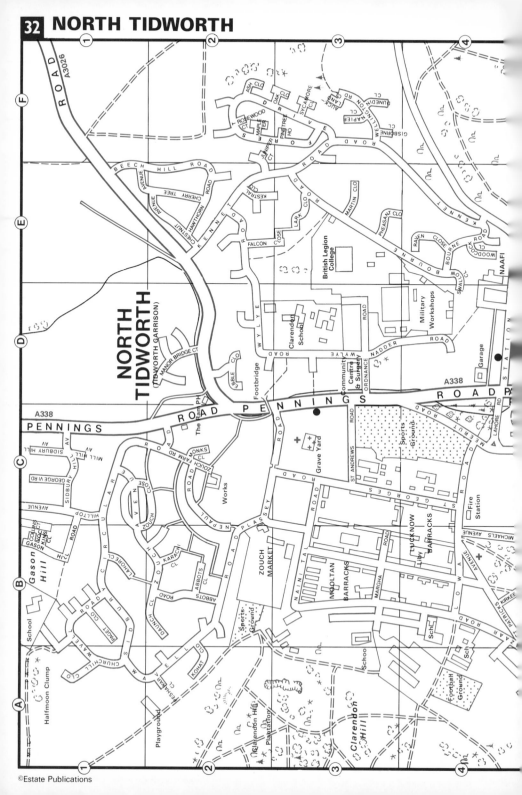

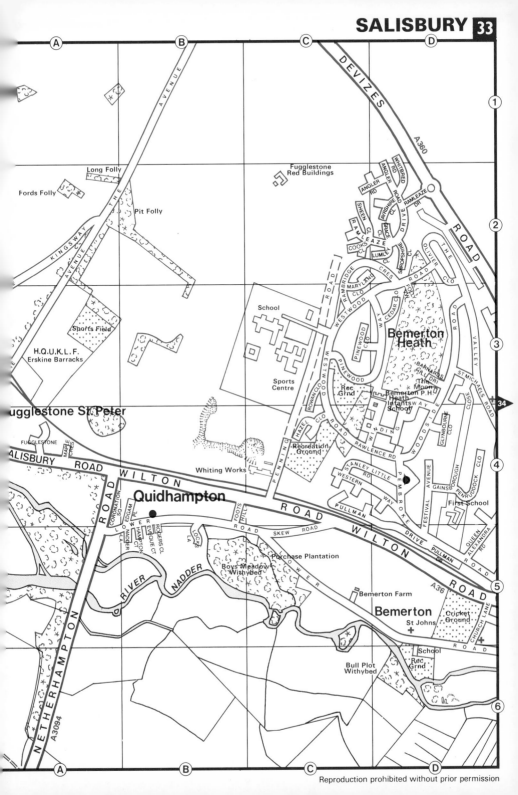

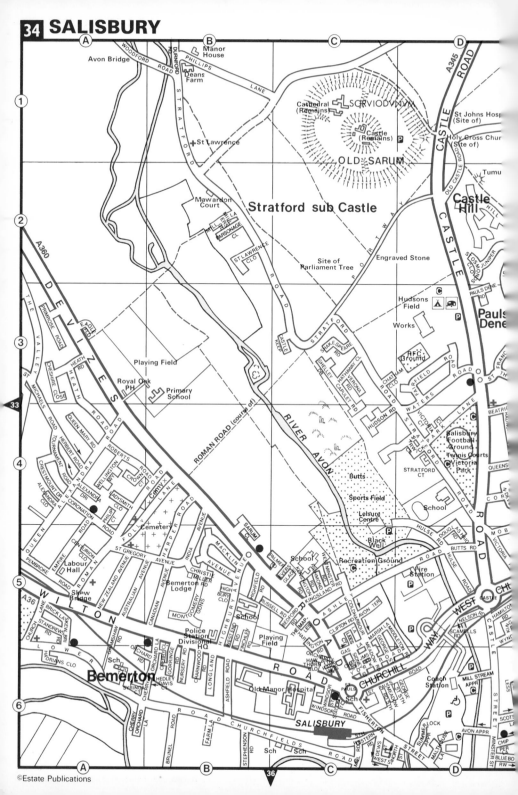

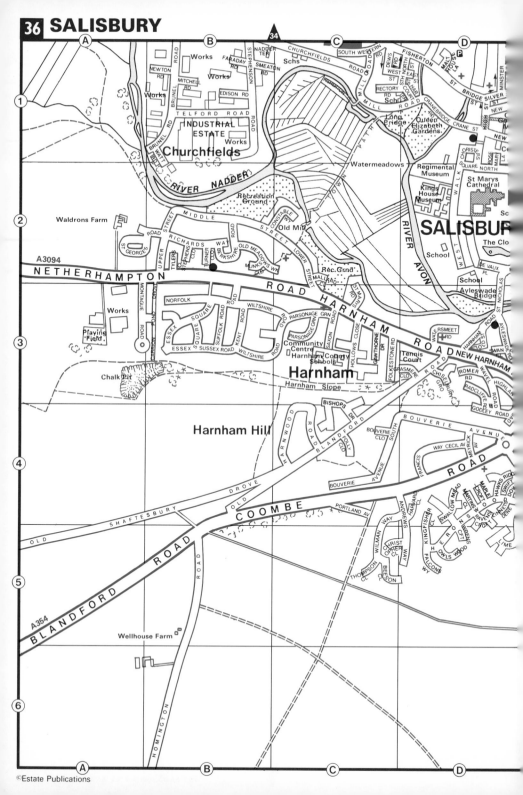

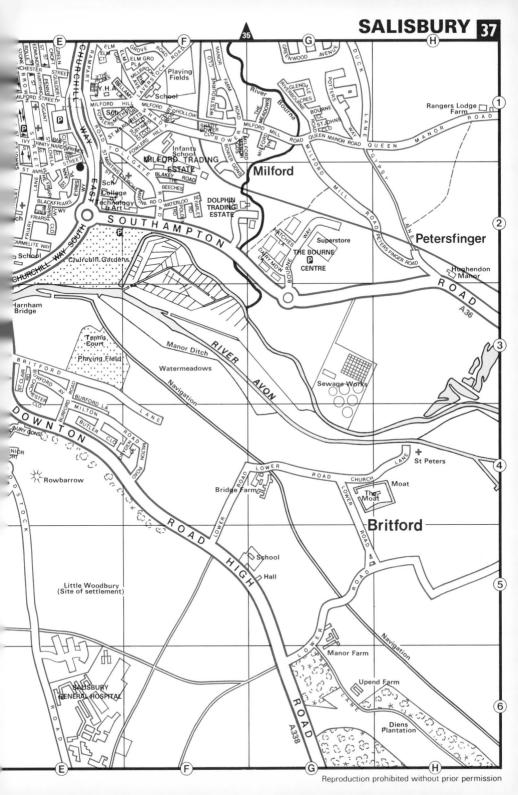

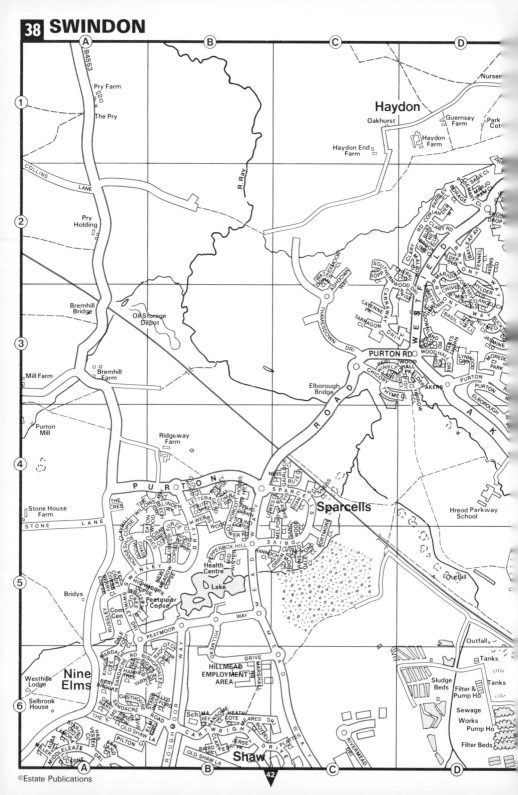

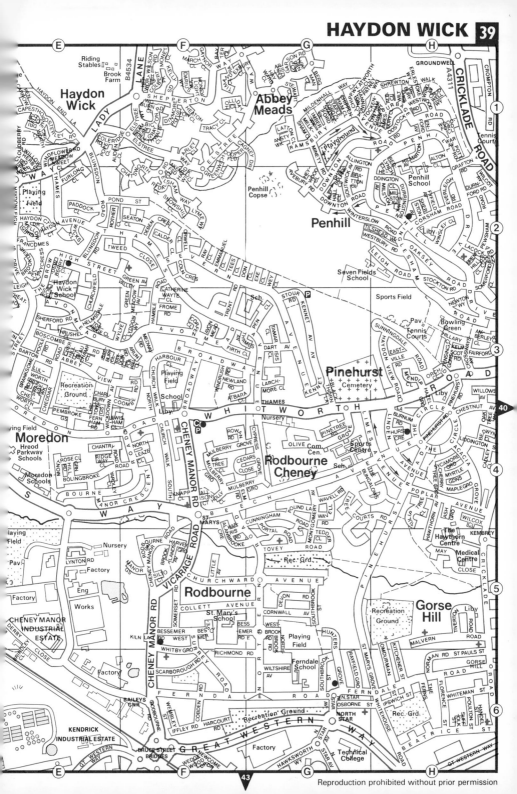

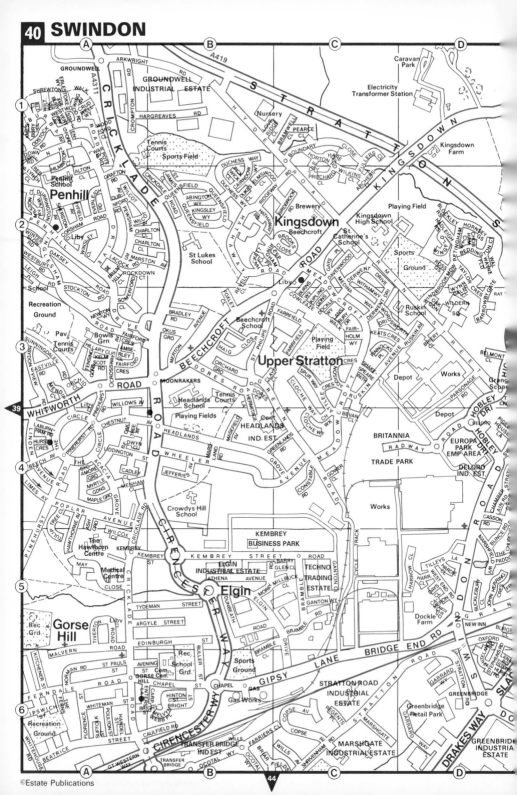

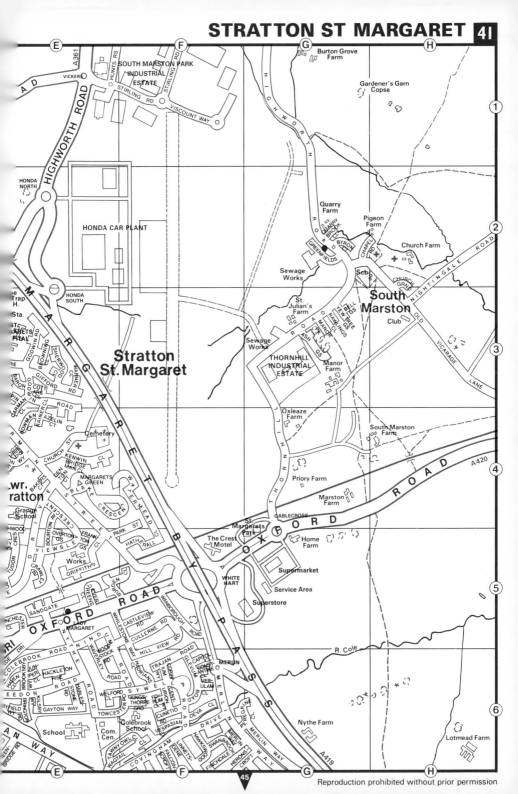

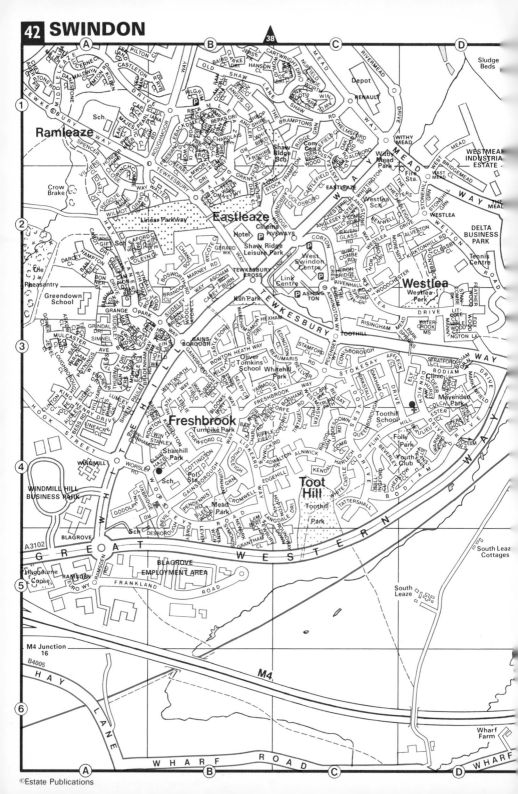

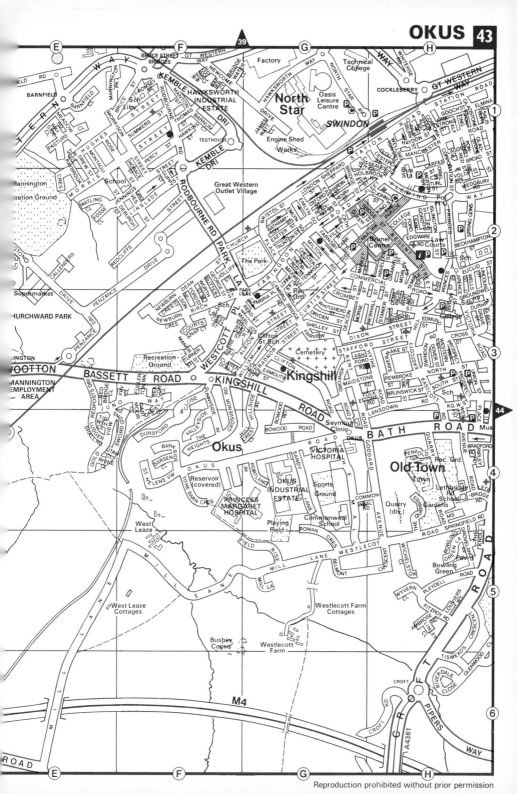

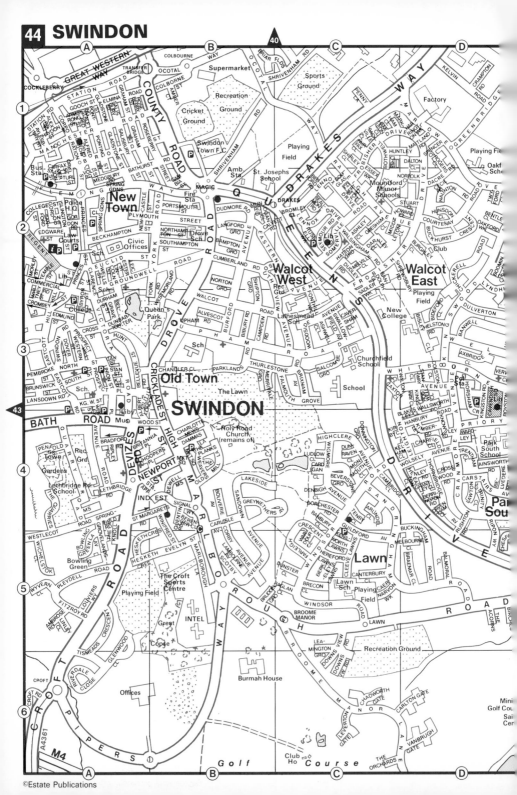

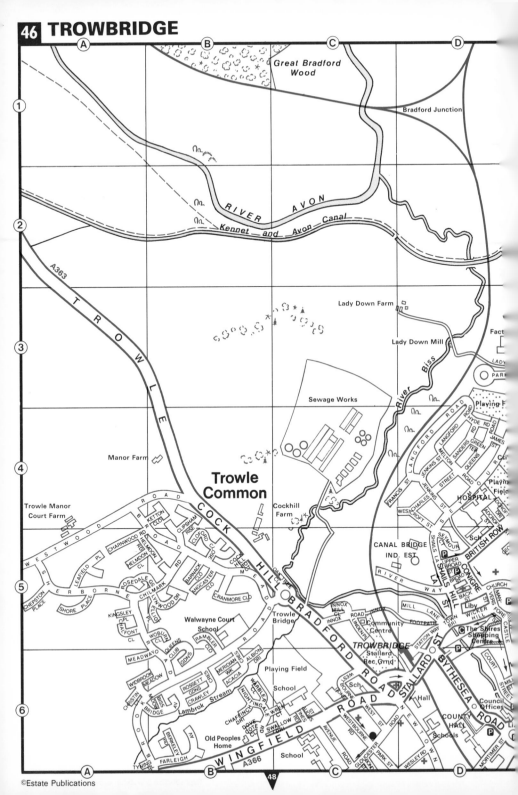

Great Bradford Wood

Bradford Junction

RIVER AVON

Kennet and Avon Canal

A363

T R O W L E

Lady Down Farm

Lady Down Mill

River Biss

Fact

LADY PARK

Playing F

Sewage Works

Manor Farm

Trowle Common

Cockhill Farm

Trowle Manor Court Farm

Chepston Place

Shore Place

WESTWOOD

SHERBORNE

LEAFIELD PL

CHARNWOOD RD

HELMDON CL

ROSEDALE

CHILMARK

ROAD

KETTON CLO

CLIPSHAM RISE

CLOFORD CLO

COCKHILL

BARNACK CLO

NAGCASTER CLO

CRANMORE CLO

Walwayne Court School

Trowle Bridge

COCK HILL

BRADFORD

ROAD

KINGSLEY PL

FALFONT CL

WOBURN CL

QUEENS

RAMBLER CLO

CLUB GDNS

MERIDIAN WK

ACACIA

ALBION DRI

WEBLEA

MEADWAYO

WIDBROOK MEADOW

ROSSETT GDNS

CRAWLEY

CRESTLN

BRIDGE

Lambrok Stream

CHAFFINCH

NIGHTINGALE

DOVE COTE

SWALLOW DRI

WREN

Old Peoples Home

BERKELEY AV

TYNING

FARLEIGH

School

WINGFIELD

A366

FRANCIS ST

JENKINS

STREET

WESTCROFT ST

LANGFORD ROAD

MELTON

CHARLES ST

SHALS LA

SEYMOUR

UPPER BROAD

RIVER

WAY

BROAD

BACK ST

HYDE RD

SANDERS

GREEN

QUEENS

JAMES

HOSPITAL

BRITISH ROW

CONIGRE

SHALS HILL

CHURCH

WICKER HILL

TOWN BRI

Liby

The Shires Shopping Centre

CASTLE

CANAL BRIDGE IND. EST

INNOX MILL ROAD

INNOX

LINDEN

Community Centre

FOOTPATH

MILL LANE

STATION WAY

TROWBRIDGE

Stallard Rec. Gmd

S3M

Sch

BOURNE

STALLARD ST

Hall

WEST ST

BYTHESEA ROAD

Council Offices

COUNTY HALL Schools

WESTBOURNE RD

BOURNE ROAD

GLOUCESTER

AVENUE

PARK ST

NEWTOWN

WESLEY RD

MORTIMER ST

Playing Field

School

Scl

Playing Field

Cli

Cl

48

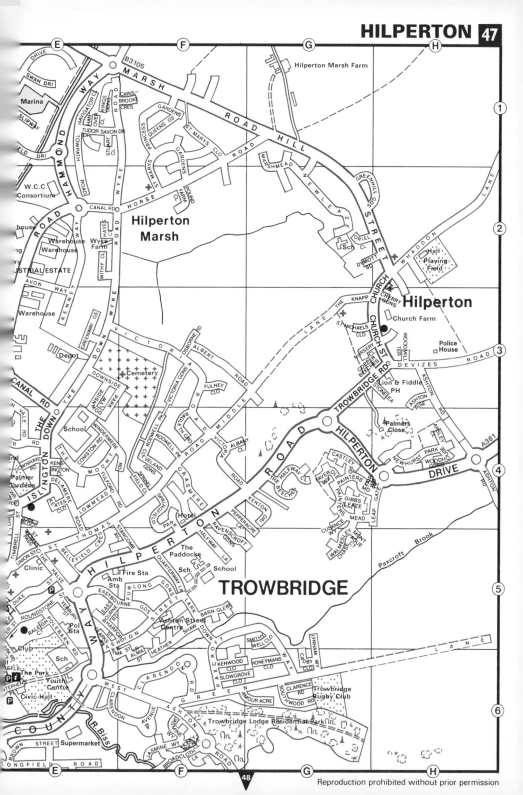

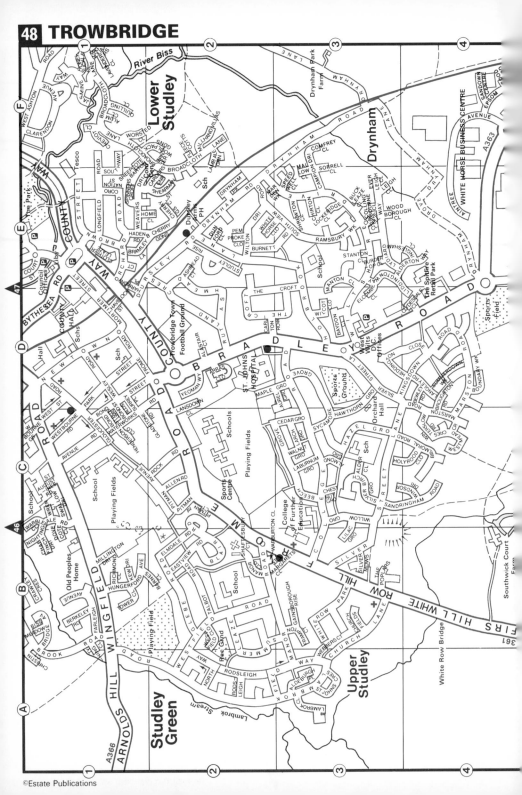

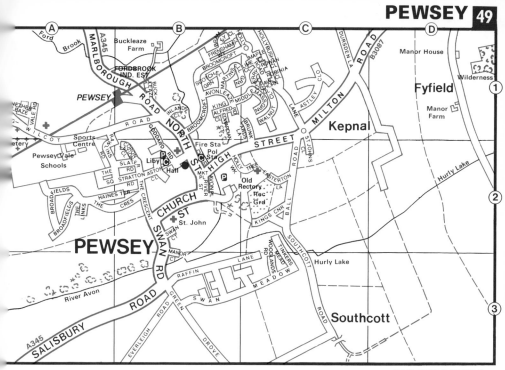

Scale 6 inches to 1 mile **TISBURY**

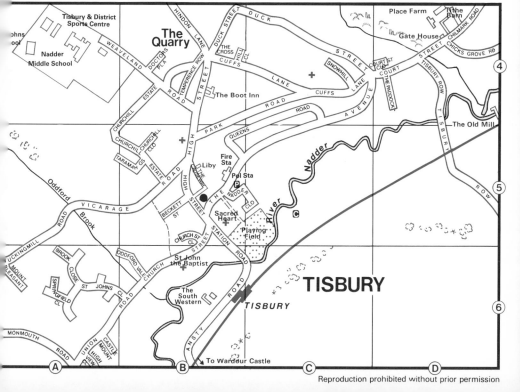

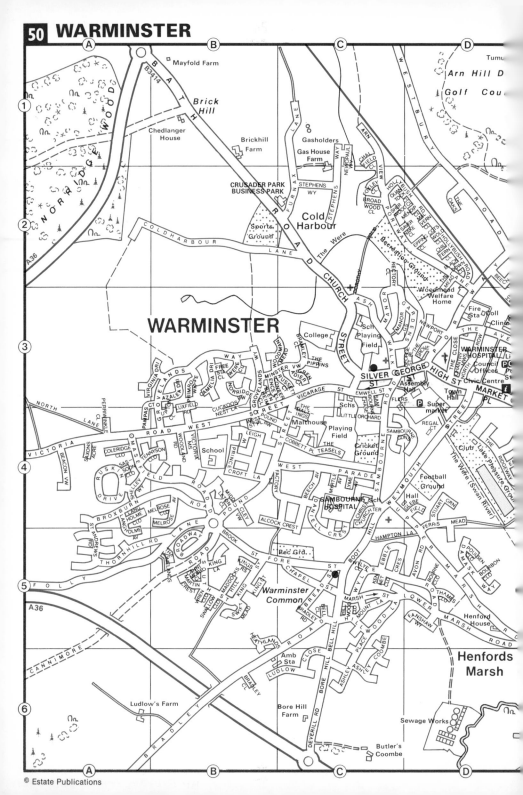

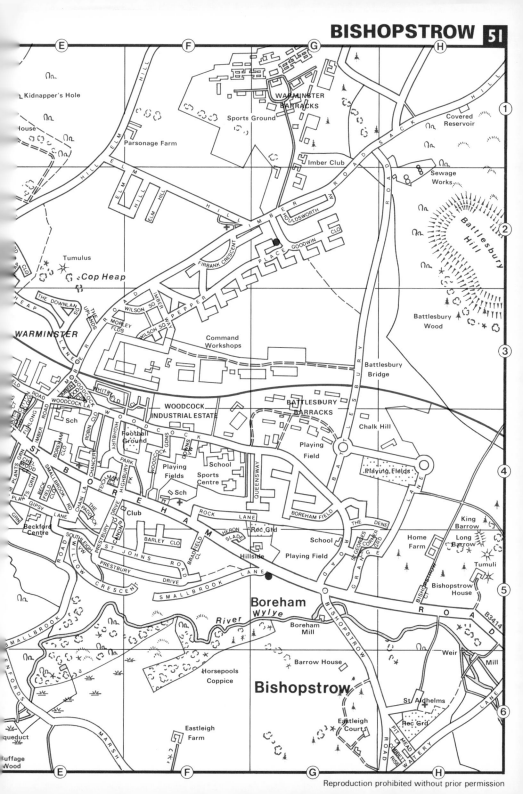

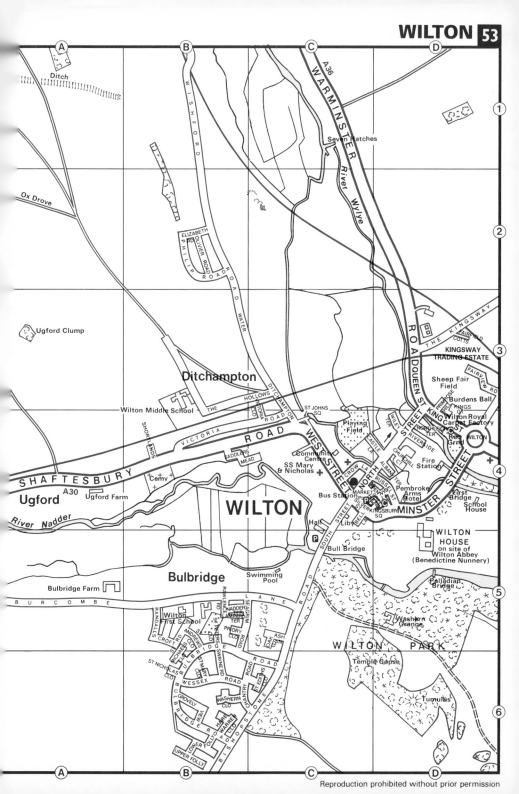

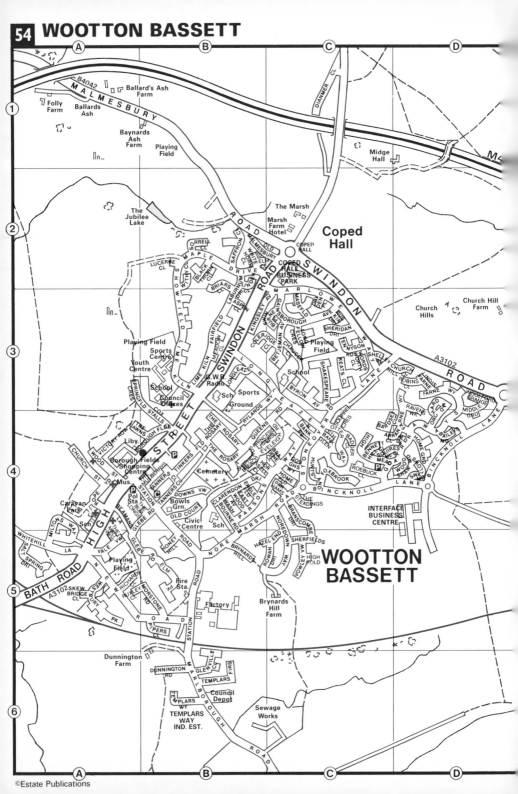

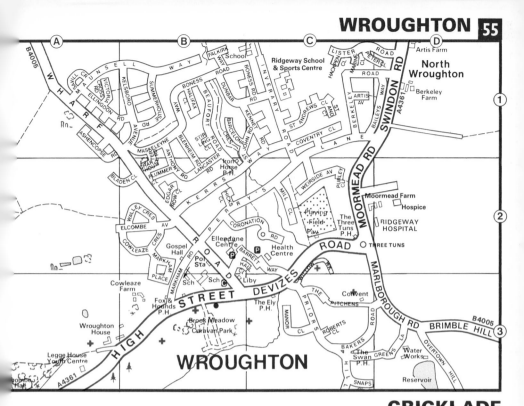

WROUGHTON

North Wroughton

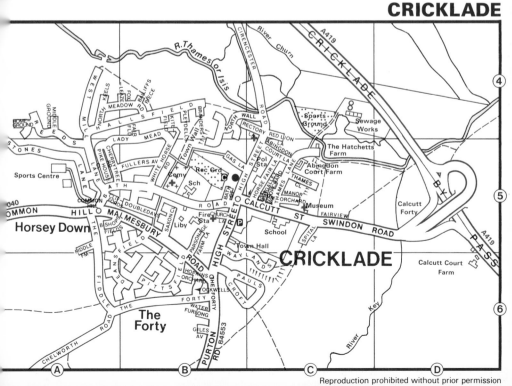

CRICKLADE

Horsey Down

The Forty

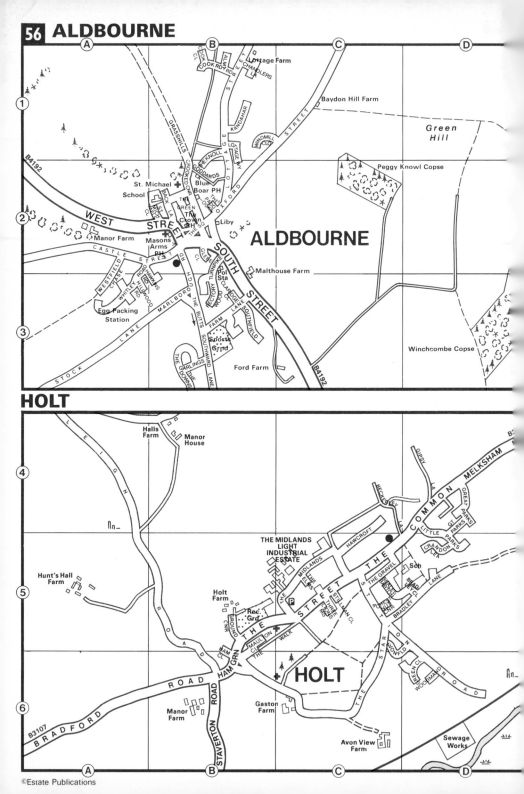

56 ALDBOURNE

ALDBOURNE

Green Hill

Cottage Farm
Baydon Hill Farm
Peggy Knowl Copse
St. Michael
School
Blue Boar PH
The Green
The Clown PH
Liby
Masons Arms PH
Manor Farm
WEST STREET
Malthouse Farm
Egg Packing Station
SOUTH STREET
Pol Sta
Sports Grnd
Ford Farm
Winchcombe Copse
CASTLE STREET
Westfield
Whitley Rd
The Butts
The Garlings
The Downs
Southfield
Southward Lane
Stock Lane
Marlboro Lane
B4192
B4192

HOLT

Halls Farm
Manor House
Hunt's Hall Farm
THE MIDLANDS LIGHT INDUSTRIAL ESTATE
Hawcroft
COMMON MELKSHAM
Great Parks
Little Parks
Sch
Holt Farm
Rec. Grd
THE STREET
THE GRAVEL
HOLT
Manor Farm
Gaston Farm
Avon View Farm
Sewage Works
BRADFORD ROAD
STAVERTON ROAD
HAM GRN
B3107

©Estate Publications

Harris Rd. SN11 16 C1
Hazel Gro. SN11 16 B5
Hazell Clo. SN11 16 C1
Heather Way. SN11 16 C5
Heron Clo. SN11 16 D3
High St. SN11 16 B3
Highgrove Clo. SN11 16 D3
Holly Clo. SN11 16 C5
Honey Garston. SN11 16 C2
Honeymead. SN11 16 C2
Horsebrook. SN11 16 C4
Horsebrook Ho. SN11 16 C4
Hungerford Rd. SN11 16 C2
INDUSTRIAL ESTATES:
Portemarsh Ind Est. SN11 16 C1
Station Rd Ind Est. SN11 16 B4
Jasmine Clo. SN11 16 C5
Keevil Av. SN11 16 A3
Kerry Cres. SN11 16 B3
Kingsbury St. SN11 16 B3
Lansdowne Clo. SN11 16 A2
Lickhill Rd. SN11 16 B1
Lilac Way. SN11 16 B5
Lime Tree Clo. SN11 16 A3
Linden Clo. SN11 16 B4
*Lodge Clo, Longbarrow Rd. SN11 16 A3
London Rd. SN11 16 C4
Longbarrow Rd. SN11 16 A3
Low La. SN11 16 C4
Luckett Way. SN11 16 C1
Macaulay Sq. SN11 16 C3
Magnolia Rise. SN11 16 B5
Mallard Clo. SN11 16 D3
Maple Clo. SN11 16 C5
Marden Way. SN11 16 B4
Market Hill. SN11 16 B3
Martin Way. SN11 16 C1
Maundrell Rd. SN11 16 C1
Meadow Vw. SN11 16 D6
Mill St. SN11 16 B3
Nestleton Clo. SN11 16 B4
New Rd. SN11 16 B3
Newcroft Clo. SN11 16 B1
Newcroft Rd. SN11 16 B1
North End. SN11 16 A2
North St. SN11 16 B2
Northcote. SN11 16 B2
Northway. SN11 16 A2
Ogilvie Sq. SN11 16 C3
Oldbury Prior. SN11 16 C5
Oldbury Way. SN11 16 A3
Orchard Clo. SN11 16 C4
Oxford Rd. SN11 16 B3
Page Clo. SN11 16 C3
Park Clo. SN11 16 D4
Patford St. SN11 16 B3
Penn Hill Rd. SN11 16 C2
Phelps Par. SN11 16 B3
Pinnhills. SN11 16 B4
Pinniger Ho. SN11 16 C3
Porte Marsh Rd. SN11 16 C1
Portland Pl. SN11 16 D4
Portland Way. SN11 16 D4
Priestley Gro. SN11 16 C4
Primrose Clo. SN11 16 B1
Prince Charles Dri. SN11 16 C3
Pym Ho. SN11 16 C3
Quarr Barton. SN11 16 B3
Quarry Dale Clo. SN11 16 C4
Ridgemead. SN11 16 B1
Riverside. SN11 16 D6
Rochdale Av. SN11 16 B1
Roundhouse. SN11 16 D5
Saddle Back Clo. SN11 16 C4
Saffron Mdw. SN11 16 A3
St Catherines Clo. SN11 16 C2
St Dunstan Clo. SN11 16 B1
St Nicholas Clo. SN11 16 C2
Sand Pit Rd. SN11 16 D1
Sandy Ridge. SN11 16 C4
Sarum Av. SN11 16 A3
Savernake Dri. SN11 16 A3
Shelburne Rd. SN11 16 C4
Silbury Rd. SN11 16 A3
Silver St. SN11 16 B5
South Pl. SN11 16 B4
Station Rd. SN11 16 B4
Stockley La. SN11 16 C6
Stokes Croft. SN11 16 B2
Swaddon St. SN11 16 B2
Tamarisk Clo. SN11 16 C5
Tern Clo. SN11 16 D3
The Glebe. SN11 16 C3
The Green. SN11 16 C4

The Knapp. SN11 16 C3
The Pippin. SN11 16 B3
The Quarry. SN11 16 B5
The Rise. SN11 16 C6
The Slades. SN11 16 C2
The Square. SN11 16 B3
The Strand. SN11 16 B3
The Wharf. SN11 16 B3
The Wynd. SN11 16 B2
Thomas Ct. SN11 16 C4
Trinity Pk. SN11 16 C5
Tyning Pk. SN11 16 C5
Valley View. SN11 16 B4
Vicarage Clo. SN11 16 C3
Victoria Ter. SN11 16 B2
*Walter Sutton Clo, Longbarrow Rd. SN11 16 A3
Wansdyke Dri. SN11 16 A3
Warren Cres. SN11 16 C2
Wenhill Heights. SN11 16 B4
Wenhill La. SN11 16 B4
Wintergreen. SN11 16 A2
Wessex Clo. SN11 16 D3
Wessington Av. SN11 16 C5
Wessington St. SN11 16 V5
Wessington Pk. SN11 16 D5
Westerham Wk. SN11 16 D4
White Horse Way. SN11 16 B5
William St. SN11 16 C1
Wood St. SN11 16 B3
Woodhill Av. SN11 16 C2
Woodhill Rise. SN11 16 C4
Woodland Pk. SN11 16 B4
Woodroffe Sq. SN11 16 C3
Wyvern Av. SN11 16 D3
Yew Tree Clo. SN11 16 A3

CHIPPENHAM

Acacia Clo. SN14 18 A2
Allington Way. SN14 18 A2
Andrews Clo. SN14 18 B4
Applewood Clo. SN14 18 C3
Arundel Clo. SN14 18 A4
Ascot Clo. SN14 18 A6
Ashe Cres. SN15 18 D1
Ashfield Rd. SN15 18 D2
Audley Rd. SN14 18 C4
Avebury Rd. SN14 18 A5
Avenue La Fleche. SN15 18 D4
Avonmead. SN15 19 F3
Awdry Clo. SN14 18 A4
Barken Rd. SN14 18 A2
Barn Clo. SN14 18 A3
Barn Owl Clo. SN14 18 B1
Barnes Rd. SN14 18 B1
Barons Mead. SN14 18 A3
Barrow Grn. SN15 19 E1
Bath Rd, Hungerdown. SN14 18 A6
Bath Rd, Lowden. SN15 18 C5
Baydons La. SN15 19 E5
Bayliffes Clo. SN15 19 G4
Beale Clo. SN14 18 A4
Beechwood Rd. SN14 18 C3
Bellinger Clo. SN15 18 D1
Berkley Clo. SN14 18 A4
Birch Gro. SN15 18 D2
Birds Marsh Vw. SN15 19 E1
Blackberry Clo. SN14 18 A1
Blackbridge Rd. SN15 19 F3
Blackcross. SN15 19 F5
Bluebell Dri. SN14 18 B1
Boothmead. SN14 18 B3
Borough Par. SN15 18 D4
Boundary Rd. SN15 19 F4
Bradbury Clo. SN15 19 G6
Brake Mead. SN15 19 F4
Bright Clo. SN15 19 F6
Brinkworth Clo. SN14 18 A4
Bristol Rd. SN14 18 A1
Brittain Clo. SN14 18 A4
Brook St. SN14 18 B3
Brookwell Clo. SN15 18 C1
Broomfield. SN15 18 D1
Brotherton Clo. SN15 19 F6
Bruges Clo. SN15 19 F4
Brunel Ct. SN14 18 B5
Bulls Hill. SN15 19 E5
Bumpers Way. SN14 18 A2
Burlands Rd. SN15 19 E5
Burleaze. SN15 18 C6
Bythebrook. SN14 18 B2

Canterbury St. SN14 18 C3
Carnarvon Clo. SN14 18 A5
Carpenter Clo. SN15 19 F6
Castlehaven Clo. SN15 19 G6
Causeway Clo. SN15 19 E5
Cavalier Ct. SN14 18 A2
Cedar Gro. SN15 19 E2
Celandine Way. SN14 18 B1
Chamberlain Rd. SN14 18 A4
Chapel La. SN14 19 E4
Charter Rd. SN15 18 D4
Cheltenham Dri. SN14 18 A4
Chelwood Clo. SN14 18 B5
Chepstow Clo. SN14 18 A6
Chester Way. SN14 18 A6
Chestnut Rd. SN14 18 C3
Cheval Clo. SN14 18 B1
Church View. SN15 18 C1
Clift Av. SN15 19 E2
Clift Ho. SN15 18 D2
Clifton Clo. SN14 18 B3
Clover Dean. SN14 18 B1
Cocklebury La. SN15 19 E1
Cocklebury Rd. SN15 19 E3
Colborne Clo. SN15 19 H6
College Clo. SN15 19 F3
Collen Clo. SN14 18 A4
Common Slip. SN15 19 E4
Coniston Rd. SN14 18 A5
Conway Rd. SN14 18 A4
Cranwell Clo. SN14 18 A6
Cricketts La. SN15 19 F6
Crown Clo. SN15 19 G6
Culverwell Rd. SN14 18 A6
Curlew Dri. SN14 18 A1
Dallas Rd. SN15 18 C3
Danes Clo. SN15 19 F6
Darcy Clo. SN15 19 F3
Deansway. SN15 18 D1
Derby Clo. SN15 19 F6
Derriads Grn. SN14 18 A4
Derriads La. SN14 18 A4
Dover St. SN14 18 C4
Down View. SN14 18 A4
Downham Mead. SN15 19 F3
Downing St. SN14 18 C3
Dummer Way. SN15 19 G6
Dyers Clo. SN15 19 G6
Eastern Av. SN15 19 F3
Easton La. SN14 18 A4
Edridge Clo. SN15 19 F3
Elmwood. SN15 18 D1
Emery La. SN15 19 E4
Erleigh Dri. SN15 18 C4
Esmead. SN15 19 F3
Evans Clo. SN15 19 E2
Fairfoot Clo. SN14 18 A5
Fallowfield Clo. SN14 18 B1
Farleigh Clo. SN14 18 A5
Farmer Clo. SN15 19 E1
Field Vw. SN15 18 D4
Fleet Rd. SN15 18 D3
Fogham Shire. SN15 18 B4
Folkestone Clo. SN14 18 A6
Forest La. SN15 19 F6
Fortune Way. SN15 19 F6
Foundry La. SN15 19 E3
Foxgrove. SN14 18 A1
Frogwell. SN14 18 A3
Frogwell Pk. SN14 18 A3
Gales Clo. SN15 19 F3
Garrick Clo. SN15 19 G3
Garth Clo. SN15 18 B1
Gascelyn Clo. SN14 18 A4
Gastons Rd. SN14 18 C3
Gipsy La. SN15 18 D5
Gladstone Rd. SN15 18 D4
Glendale Dri. SN15 19 E5
Gleneagles Clo. SN15 19 F4
Gloucester Clo. SN14 18 A5
Goldney Av. SN14 18 C4
Goodwood Way. SN14 18 A6
Greenway Av. SN15 18 D2
Greenway Ct. SN15 18 D1
Greenway Gdns. SN15 18 D1
Greenway La. SN15 18 D2
Greenway Pk . SN15 18 D2
Gundry Clo. SN15 19 F6
Habrels Clo. SN15 19 G6
Hancock Clo. SN15 19 G6
Hardenhuish Av. SN14 18 B2
Hardenhuish La. SN14 18 B2
Hardens Clo. SN15 19 F6
Hardens Mead. SN15 19 G6
Hares Patch. SN14 18 B1
Harford Clo. SN15 19 F6
Harnish Way. SN14 18 B1
Hawkins Clo. SN15 19 F6

Hawthorn Rd. SN15 19 E2
Haydock Clo. SN14 18 A6
Heathfield. SN15 19 E1
Hereford Clo. SN14 18 A6
Hewlett Clo. SN15 19 G6
High St. SN15 19 E4
Hill Corner Rd. SN15 18 D1
Hill Rise. SN15 19 E1
Hither Clo. SN14 18 A3
Hollybush Clo. SN14 18 A1
Honeybrook Clo. SN14 18 B3
Hungerdown La. SN14 18 A6
Hungerford Rd. SN15 18 D2
INDUSTRIAL ESTATES:
Bath Rd Ind Est. SN14 18 B5
Bumpus Farm Ind Est. SN14 18 A2
Greenways Business Park. SN15 18 D1
Herman Miller Ind Est. SN14 18 B6
Parsonage Way Ind Est. SN15 19 F1
Ivy La. SN15 18 D4
Ivy Rd. SN15 18 D4
Ivyfield Ct. SN15 18 D4
Jasmine Clo. SN14 18 A2
Jordan Clo. SN15 19 F6
Kelso Ct. SN14 18 A6
Kent Clo. SN14 18 A5
Kilverts Clo. SN14 18 C1
King Alfred St. SN14 18 C3
Kingham Clo. SN14 18 C4
Kingsley Rd. SN14 18 B5
Lackham Circus. SN14 18 B5
Ladds La. SN15 19 E5
Lady Coventry Rd. SN15 19 F4
Ladyfield Rd. SN15 18 B5
Laines Head. SN15 18 C1
Lamberts. SN14 18 B3
Langley Rd. SN15 19 E2
Lanhill Vw. SN14 18 B1
Lansdown Gro. SN15 19 E2
Lapwing Cres. SN15 18 B1
Laurel Dri. SN15 18 C5
Lenton Clo. SN14 18 A4
Little Down. SN14 18 B4
Little Englands. SN15 19 E5
Littlecote Rd. SN14 18 A5
Lockside. SN15 19 F6
Lodge Rd. SN15 19 G6
London Rd. SN15 19 F5
Long Clo. SN15 19 E5
Long Ridings. SN15 18 C1
Longstone. SN14 18 A2
Lords Mead. SN14 18 A3
Lovers Walk. SN15 18 D4
Lowden. SN15 18 C5
Lowden Av. SN15 18 C4
Lowden Hill. SN15 18 C4
Loyalty St. SN14 18 C4
Ludlow Clo. SN15 19 G6
Lydiard Rd. SN14 18 A5
Lytham Clo. SN15 19 F4
Malmesbury Rd. SN15 18 C1
Manor Rd. SN14 18 A3
Maple Way. SN15 18 D1
Market Pl. SN15 19 E4
Marlborough Ct. SN14 18 C4
Marshall St. SN14 18 C4
Marshfield Rd. SN14 18 C3
Martins Clo. SN15 19 G3
Matford Hill. SN15 19 G3
Maud Heaths Causeway. SN15 19 E1
Maur Clo. SN15 18 C4
Meadow Clo. SN14 18 A4
Melksham Rd. SN14 18 B6
Milestone Way. SN15 18 D1
Minster Way. SN14 18 A6
Monkton Hill. SN15 18 D4
Montague Clo. SN15 19 E1
Moorlands. SN15 19 E1
Mulberry Clo. SN15 18 B2
Murrayfield. SN15 19 E2
Neeld Cres. SN14 18 B3
New La. SN15 18 D3
New Rd. SN15 18 D3
Newall Tuck Rd. SN14 19 F4
Newbury Dri. SN14 18 A6
Northwood. SN15 19 E1
Oak Lodge Clo. SN14 18 C3
Oaklands. SN15 18 D1
Oate Hill. SN15 19 F5
Odcroft Clo. SN14 19 E1
O'Donnell Clo. SN15 19 F6

Old Hardenhuish La. SN14
Old Rd. SN15
Orchard Cres. SN14
Orchard Rd. SN14
Page Clo. SN14
Palmer St. SN14
Park Av. SN14
Park La. SN15
Park Ter. SN14
Parkfields. SN14
Parkside. SN15
Parliament St. SN14
Parsonage Way. SN15
Partridge Clo. SN15
Patchway. SN14
Pavely Clo. SN15
Pew Hill. SN15
Pewsham Lock. SN15
Pewsham Way. SN15
Pewsham Way. SN15
Picketleaze. SN14
Pipsmore Rd. SN14
Plantation. SN14
Popham Ct. SN15
Portway. SN14
Primrose Way. SN14
Queens Cres. SN14
Queens Sq. SN15
Ray Clo. SN15
Redland. SN14
Redwing Av. SN14
Ricardo Rd. SN15
Ridings Mead. SN15
Ripon Clo. SN14
River St. SN15
Riverside Dri. SN15
Robins Clo. SN14
Roman Way. SN15
Rowden Hill. SN15
Rowden La. SN15
Rowden Rd. SN15
Rowe Mead. SN15
Royal Clo. SN15
Rumble Dene. SN15
Ryan Av. SN14
Sadlers Mead. SN15
St Clements Ct. SN14
St Francis Av. SN15
St Josephs Dri. SN15
St Lukes Dri. SN15
St Margarets Gdns. SN15
St Mary St. SN15
St Marys Pl. SN15
St Mellion Clo. SN15
St Paul St. SN15
St Peters Clo. SN15
St Teresa's Dri. SN15
Salisbury Clo. SN14
Saltersford La. SN14
Sandes Clo. SN15
Sandown Dri. SN14
Sandpiper Gdns. SN14
Sarum Rd. SN14
Saxby Rd. SN15
Saxon St. SN14
School Walk. SN14
Selions Clo. SN14
Seymour Rd. SN15
Sheepscroft. SN14
Sheldon Rd. SN14
Silbury Clo. SN14
Sorrel Clo. SN14
Southmead. SN14
Southwell Clo. SN14
Spanbourn Av. SN15
Spinney Clo. SN14
Springfields Bldgs. SN15
Stainers Way. SN14
Station Hill. SN15
Stockwood Rd. SN14
Stonelea Clo. SN14
Sunningdale Clo. SN15
Sydney Wood Ct. SN14
Tall Trees. SN14
The Battens. SN14
The Bridge. SN15
The Butts. SN15
The Causeway. SN15
The Cloisters. SN15
The Firs. SN14
The Hamlet. SN15
The Oaks. SN15
The Paddocks. SN15
The Poplars. SN14
The Tinings. SN15

k Clo. SN14 18 A6
er St. SN15 19 E4
ells Pl. SN15 18 C5
Clo. SN14 18 B1
Walk. SN14 18 A5
a Rd. SN15 19 E2
berry Clo. SN15 19 F4
n Way. SN14 18 A4
kenham Way.
15 19 E2
n Rd. SN15 18 D3
St. SN14 18 C4
son View. SN15 18 C4
rs Clo. SN15 19 F4
ents Rd. SN14 18 A2
dour Rd. SN14 18 A5
rs Edge. SN15 19 E6
vern Ct. SN14 18 A4
o Clo. SN15 19 E6
bington Rd. SN15 19 E6
more Av. SN15 18 D2
s Clo. SN14 18 A6
tworth Clo. SN15 19 F4
sex Rd. SN14 18 B3
t Cepen Way. SN4 18 A1
tbrook Clo. SN14 18 A4
tcroft. SN14 18 B6
terleigh Clo. SN14 18 B5
tmead La. SN15 18 D5
tmead Ter. SN15 19 E5
tminster Gdns.
14 18 B4
herby Clo. SN14 18 A6
ttle Clo. SN14 18 A4
ks Dri. SN15 19 F6
ow Gro. SN15 19 E1
owbank. SN14 18 B2
chester Clo. SN14 18 A5
dlass Way. SN15 19 F6
dsor Clo. SN14 18 A5
hart Way. SN15 19 F6
od La. SN15 19 E5
odlands Rd. SN14 18 C4
odpecker Clo. SN14 18 B1
ndham Clo. SN15 19 F3
vstock Cres East.
N15 18 C2
vstock Cres West.
N15 18 C2
k Clo. SN14 18 A5

CORSHAM

ademy Dri. SN13 17 C2
xander Ter. SN13 17 D2
en Rd. SN13 17 A3
ley Clo. SN13 17 C3
holds Mead. SN13 17 D2
n Clo. SN13 17 C3
sil Hill Rd. SN13 17 A4
h Rd. SN13 17 A2
echfield Rd. SN13 17 C2
lott Dri. SN13 17 C3
nces La. SN13 17 E1
chel Rd. SN13 17 C3
adford Rd. SN13 17 A3
akspear Dri. SN13 17 C3
oadmead. SN13 17 F4
ook Dri. SN13 17 F4
unel Clo. SN13 17 D2
rn Rd. SN13 17 C3
arles St. SN13 17 D2
arlwood Rd. SN13 17 D3
estnut Grange. SN13 17 B2
urch St. SN13 17 E2
urchill Way. SN13 17 D1
evedale Rd. SN13 17 E4
oulston Rd. SN13 17 E1
esswells. SN13 17 D3
oss Keys Rd. SN13 17 E1
rl Croft Rd. SN13 17 B4
anvers Rd. SN13 17 C2
ckens Av. SN13 17 C2
cketts Rd. SN13 17 E4
ovecote Dri. SN13 17 C2
ridge Pl. SN13 17 C3
m Gro. SN13 17 C2
m Hayes. SN13 17 E4
neston Vw. SN13 17 D2
helred Pl. SN13 17 C2
ller Av. SN13 17 C3
rzehill. SN13 17 D3
lebe Way. SN13 17 C3
rove Rd. SN13 17 E3
ardhams Rise. SN13 17 D3
Hartham La. SN13 17 D1
Hastings Rd. SN13 17 E3
Hatton Way. SN13 17 C3
High St. SN13 17 E2
Hitherspring. SN13 17 D4
Hudswell La. SN13 17 A4
Hulbert Clo. SN13 17 C3
INDUSTRIAL ESTATES:
Park La Ind Est. SN13 17 A3
Ivy Field. SN13 17 E2
Jargeau Ct. SN13 17 E3
Kings Av. SN13 17 D1
Kirby Rd. SN13 17 C2
Lacock Rd. SN13 17 E3
Ladbrook La. SN13 17 F4
Light Clo. SN13 17 E2
Ludmead Rd. SN13 17 E4
Lypiatt Mead. SN13 17 E4
Lypiatt Rd. SN13 17 E4
Manor Rd. SN13 17 D1
Masons Way. SN13 17 B3
Mayo Clo. SN13 17 C2
Meadland. SN13 17 C2
Meriton Av. SN13 17 E2
Methuen Way. SN13 17 D1
Middlewick La. SN13 17 C1
Neale Clo. SN13 17 D2
Newlands Rd. SN13 17 E2
Nursery Gdns. SN13 17 E3
Oathills. SN13 17 D3
Oliver Av. SN13 17 D2
Orchard Rd. SN13 17 D1
Paddock La. SN13 17 B3
Park La. SN13 17 A4
Partridge Clo. SN13 17 C3
Paul St. SN13 17 D3
Peel Circus. SN13 17 B3
Penleigh Clo. SN13 17 D3
Pickwick Rd. SN13 17 C2
Pictor Clo. SN13 17 B3
Pockeredge Dri. SN13 17 A4
Pockeredge Rd. SN13 17 C4
Post Office La. SN13 17 E2
Potley La. SN13 17 C4
Pound Hill Prospect.
SN13 17 E3
Pound Mead. SN13 17 D4
Poynder Rd. SN13 17 C3
Priory New Rd. SN13 17 D2
Priory St. SN13 17 D2
Providence Rd. SN13 17 D2
Purleigh Rd. SN13 17 C2
Queens Av. SN13 17 D1
Randall Ct. SN13 17 B2
St Barbaras Rd. SN13 17 B3
Saunders Gro. SN13 17 B3
Savernake Rd. SN13 17 B4
Shearwater Way. SN13 17 B4
Sheffield La. SN13 17 B3
Silman Clo. SN13 17 B2
South St. SN13 17 E3
Southerwicks. SN13 17 D3
Spackman La. SN13 17 C3
Spring Gdns. SN13 17 E2
Spring La. SN13 17 A4
Station Rd. SN13 17 E3
Stokes Rd. SN13 17 E3
Sumsions Dri. SN13 17 B3
Swan Rd. SN13 17 C3
Syon Clo. SN13 17 C3
Tacker Clo. SN13 17 C3
Tellcroft Clo. SN13 17 D4
The Cleeve. SN13 17 E4
The Knowle. SN13 17 D3
The Laggar. SN13 17 D1
The Precinct. SN13 17 E2
The Tynings. SN13 17 D3
Tropenell Clo. SN13 17 C3
Tupman Rd. SN13 17 C2
Upper Potley. SN13 17 B4
Valley Rd. SN13 17 C2
Weller Rd. SN13 17 D2
West Park Rd. SN13 17 C2
Williams Gro. SN13 17 E3
Woodborough Rd. SN13 17 F4
Woodlands. SN13 17 C2
Yockney Clo. SN13 17 C3
York Clo. SN13 17 D1

CRICKLADE

Abingdon Ct La. SN6 55 C5
Bailiffs Piece. SN6 55 B4
Bath Ct. SN6 55 B5
Bath Rd. SN6 55 A5
Bishopsfields. SN6 55 A5
Branders. SN6 55 B4
Calcutt St. SN6 55 C5
Chelworth Rd. SN6 55 A6
Cherrytree Rd. SN6 55 A5
Church La. SN6 55 B5
Cirencester Rd. SN6 55 C4
Cliffords. SN6 55 A5
Common Hill. SN6 55 A5
Cricklade By-Pass. SN6 55 C4
Deansfield. SN6 55 A6
Doubledays. SN6 55 B5
Fairfield. SN6 55 B4
Fairview. SN6 55 C5
Fiddle Farm. SN6 55 A5
Foxleaze. SN6 55 B4
Fullers Av. SN6 55 B5
Galley Orchard. SN6 55 C5
Gas La. SN6 55 B5
Giles Av. SN6 55 B6
Hallsfield. SN6 55 A4
Hammonds. SN6 55 C5
High St. SN6 55 B5
Homeground. SN6 55 A4
Hopkins Orchard. SN6 55 B6
Horse Fair La. SN6 55 C5
Keels. SN6 55 A4
Kitefield. SN6 55 B4
Lady Mead. SN6 55 A5
Malmesbury Rd. SN6 55 A5
Manor Orchard. SN6 55 C5
Middle Ground. SN6 55 A4
North Meadow Rd.
SN6 55 A4
North Wall. SN6 55 B4
Ockwells. SN6 55 B6
Parsonage Farm La.
SN6 55 B5
Pauls Croft. SN6 55 B6
Pike House Clo. SN6 55 A5
Pittsfield. SN6 55 B6
Pleydells. SN6 55 B4
Purton Rd. SN6 55 B6
Rectory La. SN6 55 C4
Red Lion La. SN6 55 C4
Reeds. SN6 55 A4
Saxon Clo. SN6 55 B5
Spital La. SN6 55 C5
Stones La. SN6 55 A5
Swindon Rd. SN6 55 C5
Thames Clo. SN6 55 C5
Thames La. SN6 55 C5
The Fiddle. SN6 55 A5
The Forty. SN6 55 B6
Water Furlong. SN6 55 B6
Waylands. SN6 55 B6
West Mill La. SN6 55 A4
White Horse Rd. SN6 55 B5

DEVIZES

Addington Clo. SN10 21 F5
Anstie Clo. SN10 21 G3
Ash Walk. SN10 21 H1
Avon Rd. SN10 20 B4
Avon Ter. SN10 21 E3
Badgers Clo. SN10 21 F5
Bath Rd. SN10 20 A4
Beau Clerc St. SN10 20 C4
Beechfield Dri. SN10 21 H2
Beechwood Dri. SN10 21 H1
Belle Vue Rd. SN10 20 D3
Bratton Av. SN10 21 G5
Brickham Rd. SN10 21 G3
Brickley La. SN10 21 G3
Bricksteed Av. SN10 21 G4
Bridewell St. SN10 21 F4
Broadleas Clo. SN10 21 E5
Broadleas Cres. SN10 21 E5
Broadleas Pk. SN10 21 E6
Broadleas Rd. SN10 21 E5
Caen Hill Gdns. SN10 20 B4
Caird Lawns. SN10 21 G5
Canal Way. SN10 21 H2
Castle Ct. SN10 21 E4
Castle La. SN10 21 E4
Castle Rd. SN10 21 E4
Chandler Clo. SN10 21 G4
Chantry Ct. SN10 21 F3
Charles Morrison Clo.
SN10 21 E4
Charter Clo. SN10 21 G2
Church Walk. SN10 21 F4
Church Yard. SN10 21 E4
Coate La. SN10 21 H2
Colston Rd. SN10 21 E3
Commercial Rd. SN10 21 E3
Consciences La. SN10 20 B1
Coping Clo. SN10 21 F4
Cornfield Rd. SN10 21 G4
Cornwall Cres. SN10 21 E5
Couch La. SN10 21 E3
Cowslip Clo. SN10 21 H2
Cranesbill Rd. SN10 21 H2
Cromwell Rd. SN10 21 G4
Cunnington Clo. SN10 21 G3
Cygnet Clo. SN10 21 H2
Devizes Rd. SN10 20 A1
Downlands Rd. SN10 21 F6
Drakes Av. SN10 21 F5
Drews Pond La. SN10 21 F6
Dundas Clo. SN10 20 B4
Dunkirk Hill. SN10 20 C3
Dyehouse La. SN10 21 E2
Eastleigh Clo. SN10 21 G5
Eastleigh Rd. SN10 21 G5
Edward Rd. SN10 21 F5
Elcombe Gdns. SN10 21 E3
Elizabeth Dri. SN10 21 G3
Elmtree Clo. SN10 21 H5
Elmtree Gdns. SN10 21 H5
Estcourt Cres. SN10 21 F3
Estcourt Hill. SN10 21 E4
Estcourt St. SN10 21 F3
Forty Acres Rd. SN10 21 G4
Furlong Clo. SN10 20 A2
Furze Hill. SN10 20 C6
Gables Clo. SN10 21 G5
Gains La. SN10 21 F3
Granary Clo. SN10 21 G4
Granary Rd. SN10 21 G4
Great Western Clo.
SN10 21 E3
Green La. SN10 21 F6
Greenfield Rd. SN10 21 F6
Gundry Clo. SN10 21 G3
Hambleton Av. SN10 21 H1
Hare & Hounds St.
SN10 21 F4
Harebell Way. SN10 21 H2
Hartfield. SN10 21 E5
Hartmoor Rd. SN10 20 D6
High Lawn. SN10 20 C3
High St, Devizes. SN10 21 E4
High St, Rowde. SN10 20 A1
Hill Rd. SN10 21 G6
Hillworth Gdns. SN10 21 E4
Hillworth Rd. SN10 20 E4
Hodge Clo. SN10 21 H4
Hopkins Clo. SN10 21 H4
Hopton Rd. SN10 21 H1
INDUSTRIAL ESTATES:
Garden Trading Est.
SN10 21 G2
Hopton Ind Est. SN10 21 H1
Nursteed Ind Est.
SN10 21 G5
Jackson Clo. SN10 21 G5
John Rennie Clo. SN10 20 D5
John Rumble Ct. SN10 21 F4
Jump Farm Rd. SN10 21 G3
Kemp Clo. SN10 21 G3
Kempsfield. SN10 21 G6
Kennet Rd. SN10 21 G5
Kingfisher Dri. SN10 21 H1
Kingsley Gdns. SN10 21 G4
Kingsley Rd. SN10 21 G4
Kingsmanor Wharf.
SN10 21 H2
Kirby Clo. SN10 21 G3
*Lansdowne Gro,
Sheep St. SN10 21 F4
*Lansdowne Ter,
Sheep St. SN10 21 F4
Lawrence Clo. SN10 21 F6
Le Marchant Clo. SN10 21 H2
Lewis's Ct. SN10 21 E3
Linden Ter. SN10 21 F4
Little Brittox. SN10 21 E3
London Rd. SN10 21 G3
Long St. SN10 21 E4
Longcroft Av. SN10 21 G4
Longcroft Cres. SN10 21 G4
Longcroft Rd. SN10 21 G4
Longfields Walk. SN10 21 G5
Lower Wharf. SN10 21 E3
Market Pl. SN10 21 E3
Marsh La. SN10 20 A1
Maryport St. SN10 21 F4
Maslen Clo. SN10 21 H4
Matilda Way. SN10 21 G2
Mattock Clo. SN10 21 G3
Maud Clo. SN10 21 G2
Maundrell Clo. SN10 20 A1
Mayenne Pl. SN10 20 B4
Meadow Dri. SN10 21 G3
Meads Pl. SN10 21 F4
Mill Clo. SN10 21 G6
Monday Market St.
SN10 21 F3
Moonrakers. SN10 21 H2
Morris La. SN10 21 F4
Moyne Clo. SN10 20 D3
Neate Rd. SN10 21 G3
New Park Rd. SN10 21 E3
New Park St. SN10 21 E3
Northgate Gdns. SN10 21 E3
Northgate St. SN10 21 E3
Nursteed Clo. SN10 21 H5
Nursteed Pk. SN10 21 G5
Nursteed Rd. SN10 21 F4
Oamaru Way. SN10 21 G4
Offers Ct. SN10 21 F4
Orchard Clo. SN10 21 F6
Pans La. SN10 21 F4
Park Vw. SN10 20 C4
Parkfields. SN10 21 G2
Phillip Clo. SN10 21 G3
Pines Rd. SN10 21 G4
Potterne Rd. SN10 21 E6
Prince Maurice Ct.
SN10 21 H1
Proudman Rd. SN10 21 H3
Quakers Walk. SN10 21 F3
Quarry Clo. SN10 21 G4
Queens Rd. SN10 21 E5
Radnor Clo. SN10 21 F5
Redhorn Gdns. SN10 21 F5
Reed Clo. SN10 21 H4
Rendells Ct. SN10 21 F4
Roseland Av. SN10 21 G4
Rotherstone. SN10 21 E3
Roundway Gdns. SN10 21 F1
Roundway Pk. SN10 21 F1
Roundway Rd. SN10 21 H1
Rowde Court Rd. SN10 20 A1
Royal Oak Ct. SN10 21 E3
St Bridget Clo. SN10 21 H4
*St Johns Ct
Church Yd. SN10 21 E4
St Johns St. SN10 21 E4
St Josephs Rd. SN10 20 D3
Salisbury St. SN10 20 C4
Sarum Dri. SN10 21 F5
Sedgefield Gdns. SN10 21 F3
Shackleton Rd. SN10 21 H5
Sheep St. SN10 21 F4
Sheppard Clo. SN10 21 E3
Sidmouth St. SN10 21 F4
Snuff St. SN10 21 E3
Southbroom Rd. SN10 21 F4
Southgate. SN10 21 F5
Southgate Clo. SN10 21 F5
Springers Clo. SN10 21 G3
Springfield Rd. SN10 20 A1
Stanley Ter. SN10 21 F5
Station Rd. SN10 20 E3
Steele Clo. SN10 21 G3
Stockwell Rd. SN10 21 G3
Sussex Wharf. SN10 20 D3
Sutton Pl. SN10 21 F4
Tanis. SN10 20 B1
The Ark. SN10 21 E4
The Breach. SN10 21 F5
The Brittox. SN10 21 E4
The Croft. SN10 21 G3
The Fairway. SN10 21 E6
The Moorlands. SN10 21 E5
The Nursery. SN10 20 D3
The Patchway. SN10 21 H4
The Sidings. SN10 20 D4
Tilley Clo. SN10 21 G3
Tintern Rd. SN10 21 F6
Tornio Clo. SN10 21 H2
Victoria Rd. SN10 21 F3
Waiblingen Way. SN10 20 D3
Walden Lodge Clo.
SN10 21 F5
Waylands. SN10 21 G4
Wessex Clo. SN10 21 G4
West View Cres. SN10 20 D4
Wharf St. SN10 21 E3
Whistley Rd. SN10 20 A4
Wick La. SN10 21 E5
Wickfield. SN10 21 F5
William Rd. SN10 21 G5
Willow Dri. SN10 21 H2
Windsor Dri. SN10 21 G3
Wine St. SN10 21 E4

Woodland Way. SN10 21 E6

DOWNTON & REDLYNCH

Apple Tree Clo. SP5 23 F3
Appletree Rd. SP5 23 F3
Avon Meadow. SP5 22 C3
Avondyke. SP5 22 B4
Barford La. SP5 22 C1
Barnaby Clo. SP5 22 A3
Batten Rd. SP5 22 A2
Bennett Clo. SP5 23 F4
Besomers Drove. SP5 23 H5
Bowers Hill. SP5 23 G3
Braemore Rd. SP5 22 A5
Castle Meadow. SP5 22 C3
Castle Woods. SP5 23 F4
Catherine Cres. SP5 22 A3
Chalks Clo. SP5 23 F3
Chapel Rd. SP5 23 G4
Church Hatch. SP5 22 C2
Church Hill. SP5 23 H4
Cranbury Clo. SP5 22 C4
Crossways Clo. SP5 22 A2
Dairy Clo. SP5 23 F5
Downlands Clo. SP5 22 C4
Downton Hill. SP5 23 F3
Eastmans Clo. SP5 22 C3
Elizabeth Clo. SP5 22 A3
Elmfield Clo. SP5 23 F5
Forest Rd. SP5 23 F6
Goggs La. SP5 23 H4
Gravel Clo. SP5 22 B1
Green La. SP5 22 C2
Greenacres. SP5 22 A2
Greens Mead. SP5 23 F4
Grove La. SP5 23 G3
Hamilton Park. SP5 22 C2
Hart Hill Drove. SP5 23 G4
Herbert Rd. SP5 23 F4
High St. SP5 22 C2
Highfield La. SP5 23 F5
Hyde La. SP5 22 A3
INDUSTRIAL ESTATES:
Batten Rd Ind Est. SP5 22 A2
Joanna Clo. SP5 22 A3
Kiln La. SP5 23 G3
Kingsford Clo. SP5 23 F5
Langford La. SP5 23 F2
Little Woodfalls Dri. SP5 23 F5
Lode Hill. SP5 22 D2
Lodge Drove. SP5 23 F6
Long Clo. SP5 22 A2
Marie Av. SP5 22 A3
Mitchells Clo. SP5 23 F4
Moot Clo. SP5 22 C3
Moot Gdns. SP5 22 B4
Moot La. SP5 22 B4
Morgans Rise Rd. SP5 23 F3
Morgans Vale Rd. SP5 23 F4
Muddyford La. SP5 23 F3
Orchard Rd. SP5 23 F3
Petticoat La. SP5 23 F5
Pine View Clo. SP5 23 F5
Primrose La. SP5 23 E4
Princes Clo. SP5 23 G3
Princes Hill. SP5 23 G3
Quavey Rd. SP5 23 G3
Roman Meadow. SP5 22 C3
Rosedene. SP5 23 G4
St Birinus Rd. SP5 23 F4
St Marys Clo. SP5 23 H5
Salisbury Rd. SP5 22 A1
Sandy La. SP5 23 G2
Saxon Meadow. SP5 22 C3
Saxonhurst. SP5 22 C3
School Rd. SP5 23 H6
Slab La. SP5 22 D2
Snail Creep. SP5 22 C2
South La. SP5 22 C2
Springfield Cres. SP5 23 F5
Squarey Clo. SP5 22 C4
The Borough. SP5 22 B2
The Close. SP5 23 F3
The Drove. SP5 23 F5
The Headlands. SP5 22 A2
The Ridge. SP5 23 F6
The Row. SP5 23 G3
The Sidings. SP5 22 D2
Tinneys Clo. SP5 23 F6
Twynham Clo. SP5 22 C3
Vale Rd. SP5 23 F4
Valley Clo. SP5 23 F4
Vicarage Pk. SP5 23 F4
Waterside. SP5 22 C3
Wheelwright Mews. SP5 22 A2
Whiteshoot. SP5 23 H6
Whiteshoot Hill. SP5 23 F6
Wick La. SP5 22 A2

DURRINGTON/ BULFORD

Addison Sq. SP4 24 B2
Alberta Gdns. SP4 24 F3
Andrew Clo. SP4 24 B2
Ann Cres. SP4 24 B2
Avondown Rd. SP4 24 C2
Birchwood Dri. SP4 24 C2
Bulford Driveway. SP4 24 C2
Bulford Droveway. SP4 24 D3
Bulford Hill. SP4 24 C3
Bulford Rd,
  Bulford. SP4 24 E2
Bulford Rd,
  Durrington. SP4 24 B1
Camellia Clo. SP4 24 D3
Charles Rd. SP4 24 B2
Church La. SP4 24 D3
Church St. SP4 24 B1
Churchill Av. SP4 24 D3
Clayton Rd. SP4 24 E3
College Rd. SP4 24 B1
Coronation Rd. SP4 24 B2
Countess Rd. SP4 24 A3
Crescent Rd. SP4 24 D3
Cygnet Dri. SP4 24 C2
Dorset Clo. SP4 24 E3
Double Hedges. SP4 24 D4
Downland Way. SP4 24 A2
Downleaze. SP4 24 B1
Dukes Way. SP4 24 E3
Elizabeth Rd. SP4 24 B2
Glebe Rd. SP4 24 B1
Glendale Rd. SP4 24 C2
Greenland Clo. SP4 24 B2
Hackthorn Rd. SP4 24 A1
Hampshire Clo. SP4 24 E3
Herons Walk. SP4 24 C2
High St, Bulford. SP4 24 D3
High St,
  Durrington. SP4 24 B1
John French Way. SP4 24 E3
Kingfisher Dri. SP4 24 C2
Larkhill Rd. SP4 24 A2
Latchmere Lodge. SP4 24 C2
Ledger Hill Clo. SP4 24 D3
Lily Walk. SP4 24 C2
Longfield Clo. SP4 24 A1
Mackenzie Gdns. SP4 24 F3
Maple Way. SP4 24 A1
Marina Clo. SP4 24 B2
Marina Cres. SP4 24 A2
Marina Rd. SP4 24 A2
Meadow Rd. SP4 24 E3
Meads Rd. SP4 24 B2
Milston Rd. SP4 24 D1
Milston Vw. SP4 24 C1
Netheravon Rd. SP4 24 A2
New Rd. SP4 24 B2
Newmans Way. SP4 24 E3
Old Barns Way. SP4 24 B1
Old Coach Rd. SP4 24 D3
Old Ward Rd. SP4 24 F3
Ontario Gdns. SP4 24 F3
Orchard End. SP4 24 D3
Philip Rd. SP4 24 B2
Pinckneys Way. SP4 24 A2
Poores Rd. SP4 24 B2
Recreation Rd. SP4 24 C1
Reed Walk. SP4 24 B1
Ridgmount. SP4 24 B1
River Way. SP4 24 C1
Robin Hill La. SP4 24 D3
St Leonards Clo. SP4 24 D3
Salisbury Rd. SP4 24 D4
School Dri. SP4 24 B2
School Rd. SP4 24 C1
Station Ter. SP4 24 A2
Stonehenge Rd. SP4 24 A2
Swan Clo. SP4 24 E3
Swattons Clo. SP4 24 E3
The Avenue. SP4 24 B1
The Ham. SP4 24 B1
The Leaze. SP4 24 B1
Vancouver Gdns. SP4 24 F3
Water St. SP4 24 C4
Watergate La. SP4 24 C4
Westfield Clo. SP4 24 A2
Willow Dri. SP4 24 A1
Wiltshire Clo. SP4 24 A1
Windsor Mews. SP4 24 B1
Windsor Rd. SP4 24 B1
Winnipeg Gdns. SP4 24 F3
Yew Tree Clo. SP4 24 C2

HIGHWORTH

Arran Way. SN6 25 A2
Barra Clo. SN6 25 A3
Biddel Springs. SN6 25 C3
Blandford Alley. SN6 25 B4
Botany. SN6 25 A4
Brewery St. SN6 25 B4
Brookfield. SN6 25 B2
Bute Clo. SN6 25 B2
Byde Mill Gdns. SN6 25 A4
Cherry Orchard. SN6 25 C3
Church Vw. SN6 25 B4
Crane Furlong. SN6 25 B2
Cricklade Rd. SN6 25 A4
Downs View. SN6 25 C3
Eastrop. SN6 25 C4
Edencroft. SN6 25 C2
Folly Clo. SN6 25 C2
Folly Cres. SN6 25 B2
Folly Dri. SN6 25 B2
Folly Way. SN6 25 C2
Grange Clo. SN6 25 C4
Grove Hill. SN6 25 B2
Grove Orchard. SN6 25 B2
Henley Dri. SN6 25 B2
High St. SN6 25 B4
Home Farm. SN6 25 A3
INDUSTRIAL ESTATES:
Blackworth Ind Est. SN6 25 B1
Islay Cres. SN6 25 B3
Kilda Rd. SN6 25 A2
Kings Av. SN6 25 C2
Knowlands. SN6 25 C2
Lechlade Rd. SN6 25 B4
Lismore Rd. SN6 25 A3
Market Pl. SN6 25 C4
Middi Haines Ct. SN6 25 C3
Newburgh Pl. SN6 25 B3
North Vw. SN6 25 B4
Oak Dri. SN6 25 B4
Orange Clo. SN6 25 C3
Park Av. SN6 25 C4
Parsonage Ct. SN6 25 C4
Pentylands Clo. SN6 25 B2
Pentylands La. SN6 25 B1
Pound Rd. SN6 25 B2
Priory Grn. SN6 25 C3
Quarry Cres. SN6 25 B3
Queens Av. SN6 25 C2
Rivers Pl. SN6 25 B3
Roman Way. SN6 25 B4
Round Hills Mead. SN6 25 C1
St Michaels Av. SN6 25 A3
Sevenfields. SN6 25 C2
Sheep St. SN6 25 B4
Shrivenham Rd. SN6 25 C5
Skye Clo. SN6 25 A2
Spa Clo. SN6 25 C3
Stapleton Clo. SN6 25 B4
Station Rd. SN6 25 B3
Stonefield Dri. SN6 25 B5
Stroma Way. SN6 25 A2
Swindon Rd. SN6 25 B6
Swindon St. SN6 25 B4
The Cullerns. SN6 25 C3
The Dormers. SN6 25 C3
The Elms. SN6 25 B4
The Green. SN6 25 B4
The Mews. SN6 25 C4
The Paddocks. SN6 25 C4
The Willows. SN6 25 C4
Turnpike Rd. SN6 25 C3
Vicarage La. SN6 25 B3
Vorda Rd. SN6 25 C2
Wessex Way. SN6 25 D2
Westhill Clo. SN6 25 B4
Westrop. SN6 25 B3
Windrush. SN6 25 A3
Wrde Hill. SN6 25 A4

HOLT

Avonfield. BA14 56 D6
Beales Barton. BA14 56 C5
Beckerley La. BA14 56 C4
Bradford Rd. BA14 56 A6
Bradley Clo. BA14 56 D5
Bradley La. BA14 56 C5
Chestnut Corner. BA14 56 C5
Crandon Lea. BA14 56 D5
Gipsy La. BA14 56 D4
Great Parks. BA14 56 D4
Green Clo. BA14 56 D6
Ground Corner. BA14 56 B5
Ham Clo. BA14 56 B6
Ham Grn. BA14 56 B6
Hawcroft. BA14 56 C5
INDUSTRIAL ESTATES:
The Midlands Light
  Ind Est. BA14 56 C5
Leigh Rd. BA14 56 A4
Little Parks. BA14 56 D4
Maulton Clo. BA14 56 B6
Melksham Rd. BA14 56 D4
Station Rd. BA14 56 C5
Staverton Rd. BA14 56 B6
Stillman Clo. BA14 56 C5
The Common. BA14 56 C5
The Elms. BA14 56 C5
The Gravel. BA14 56 C5
The Midlands. BA14 56 C5
The Star. BA14 56 C6
The Street. BA14 56 B5
The Walk. BA14 56 B6
Three Lions Mws. BA14 56 C5
Woodman. BA14 56 D6

LYNEHAM

Argosy Rd. SN15 26 D2
Arnhem Cross. SN15 26 D2
Ash Clo. SN15 26 D2
Bakers Field. SN15 26 C1
Belfast Mead. SN15 26 D2
Bradenstoke Rd. SN15 26 A1
Britannia Cres. SN15 26 D2
Calne Rd. SN15 26 C2
Church La. SN15 26 C2
Comet Clo. SN15 26 D2
Dixon Rd. SN15 26 C3
Eider Av. SN15 26 C3
Elm Clo. SN15 26 D2
End Clo. SN15 26 C2
Harrow Gro. SN15 26 C2
Hastings Dri. SN15 26 C2
Hilmarton Rd. SN15 26 B1
Hocketts Clo. SN15 26 B1
Lancaster Sq. SN15 26 C2
Lime Clo. SN15 26 D2
Mallard Av. SN15 26 C3
Muscovey Clo. SN15 26 C2
Pintail Ct. SN15 26 C3
Portal Pl. SN15 26 C3
Pound Clo. SN15 26 C1
Preston La. SN15 26 C2
Preston Vale. SN15 26 D3
St Michaels Clo. SN15 26 B1
Sheld Dri. SN15 26 C3
Slessor Rd. SN15 26 C3
Sycamore Clo. SN15 26 D2
Teal Av. SN15 26 C2
The Green. SN15 26 B1
Trenchard Rd. SN15 26 C3
Victoria Dri. SN15 26 D3
Webbs Ct. SN15 26 C1
York Rd. SN15 26 D2

MALMESBURY

Abbey Row. SN16 27 B4
Abbots Gdns. SN16 27 B4
Alexander Rd. SN16 27 A3
Amberley Ct. SN16 27 A5
Arches La. SN16 27 B5
Athelstan Rd. SN16 27 B3
Aubrey Rise. SN16 27 C1
Avon Rd. SN16 27 A3
Back Hill. SN16 27 C4
Barley Clo. SN16 27 C5
Baskerville Hill. SN16 27 C4
Blicks Hill. SN16 27 D3
Bonners Clo. SN16 27 C2
Bremilham Rise. SN16 27 A4
Bremilham Rd. SN16 27 B3
Bristol St. SN16 27 B4
Buettell Way. SN16 27 B4
Burnham Rd. SN16 27 B3
Burnivale. SN16 27 B4
Chippenham Rd. SN16 27 C6
Chubb Clo. SN16
Cirencester Rd. SN16
Common Rd. SN16
Coopers Clo. SN16
Corn Gastons. SN16
Cowbridge Cres. SN16
Cricklade Rd. SN16
Cross Hayes. SN16
Cross Hayes La. SN16
Dark La. SN16
Elmer Clo. SN16
Filands. SN16
Forrester Pl. SN16
Foundary Rd. SN16
Foxley Rd. SN16
Gastons Rd. SN16
Gloucester Rd. SN16
Gloucester St. SN16
Glovers Ct. SN16
Haddons Clo. SN16
Hanks Clo. SN16
Harpers La. SN16
High St. SN16
Hobbes Clo. SN16
Hodge La. SN16
Holford Rise. SN16
Holloway. SN16
Horse Fair. SN16
Hudson Rd. SN16
INDUSTRIAL ESTATES:
Gloucester Rd Ind Est. SN16
Malmesbury Business Pk. SN16
Ingram St. SN16
John Betjeman Clo. SN16
Katifer La. SN16
Kembles Clo. SN16
Kings Walk. SN16
Kings Wall. SN16
Lacemakers Rd. SN16
Leland Clo. SN16
Malmesbury By-Pass. SN16
Market Cres. SN16
Michael Pyms Rd. SN16
Milbourne La. SN16
Mill La. SN16
Moffatt Rise. SN16
Morse Clo. SN16
Newton Gro. SN16
Niebull Clo. SN16
Old Alexander Rd. SN16
Old Railway Clo. SN16
Olivers La. SN16
Orchard Ct. SN16
Orwell Clo. SN16
Oxford St. SN16
Park Mead. SN16
Park Rd. SN16
Parklands. SN16
Parliament Row. SN16
Pool Gastons Rd. SN16
Powell Rise. SN16
Reeds Farm Rd. SN16
River View. SN16
Ron Golding Clo. SN16
St Aldhelms Rd. SN16
St Dennis Rd. SN16
St John St. SN16
St Marys St. SN16
School La. SN16
Sherston Rd. SN16
Silver St. SN16
Silverston Way. SN16
Swindon Rd. SN16
Tetbury Rd. SN16
The Hawthorns. SN16
The Maltings. SN16
The Mews. SN16
The Old Orchard. SN16
Twynnoy Clo. SN16
Water Meadows. SN16
Weavers Clo. SN16
Webbs Way. SN16
West St. SN16
White Lion Pk. SN16
Willow View Clo. SN16
Wortheys Clo. SN16
Wychurch Rd. SN16

MARLBOROUGH

Alexandra Ter. SN8 28 D

rce Way. SP1 35 F2
nbroke Rd. SP2 33 D4
ning Rd. SP2 33 C2
nyfarthing St. SP1 37 E1
ruddock Clo. SP2 33 D4
ers Finger Rd. SP1 37 H2
lip Ct. SP1 34 A4
llips La. SP1 34 B1
grims Mead. SP1 35 F2
ewood Clo. SP2 33 C3
ewood Way. SP2 33 C3
den Rd. SP1 37 F2
olar Way. SP1 35 F2
rtland Av. SP2 36 C4
rtway. SP1 34 C2
tters Way. SP1 37 G1
mrose Rd. SP2 34 A3
llman Dri. SP2 33 C4

een Alexandra Rd.
SP2 34 A5
een Manor Rd. SP1 37 G1
een Mary Rd. SP2 34 A4
een St. SP1 37 E1
eens La. SP1 35 E5
eensberry Rd. SP1 34 D4

adcliffe Rd. SP2 36 D3
adnor Rd. SP1 34 D4
ambridge Cres. SP2 33 C3
amleaze Dri. SP2 33 C2
ampart Rd. SP1 35 E6
avenscroft. SP2 36 D4
awlence Rd. SP2 33 C4
ectory Rd. SP2 36 C1
edford Clo. SP1 35 F4
ichards Way. SP2 36 B2
ichmond Rd. SP2 34 C5
idgeway Rd. SP1 35 E5
iverbourne Rd. SP1 37 G1
iverside Clo. SP1 35 G5
iverside Rd. SP1 35 F6
oberts Rd. SP2 34 A4
ogers Clo. SP2 33 B5
ollestone St. SP1 35 E6
oman Rd. SP2 34 A5
omer Rd. SP2 36 D3
osemary Clo. SP1 35 G6
osemary La. SP1 36 D1
ougemont Clo. SP1 35 E6
owan Clo. SP2 33 C3
ussell Rd. SP2 34 B5

St Albans Clo. SP1 35 G2
St Andrews. SP1 35 G5
St Andrews Rd. SP2 34 A5
St Anns St. SP1 37 E2
St Bedes Clo. SP1 35 G2
St Brendans Clo. SP1 35 F2
St Christophers Clo. SP1 35 F2
St Clair Rd. SP1 37 E3
St Clements Way. SP1 35 F2
St Davids Clo. SP1 35 G3
St Edmunds Church St.
SP1 35 E6
St Francis Cres. SP1 35 F1
St Francis Rd. SP1 34 D3
St Georges Rd. SP2 36 A2
St Gregory Av. SP2 34 A5
St James Clo. SP1 35 G2
St Johns Clo. SP1 37 G1
St Johns St. SP1 37 E1
St Josephs Clo. SP1 35 F2
St Judes Clo. SP1 35 G3
St Lawrence Clo. SP2 34 B2
St Lukes Clo. SP1 35 G2
St Margarets Clo. SP1 37 F1
St Marks Av. SP1 35 E4
St Marks Rd. SP1 35 E5
St Martins Church St.
SP1 37 E1
St Marys Rd. SP2 36 C3
St Matthews Clo. SP2 35 G2
St Michaels Rd. SP2 33 D3
St Nicholas Rd. SP1 36 D3
St Osmonds Clo. SP1 34 D2
St Pauls Rd. SP1 34 C6
St Peters Rd. SP1 35 F2
St Teresas Clo. SP1 35 F2
St Thomas Way. SP1 35 G2
St Ursulas Clo. SP1 35 F2
Salisbury Rd. SP2 33 A4
Salt La. SP1 35 E6
Sarum Clo. SP2 34 B5
Saxon Rd. SP1 36 C3
Scamells Rd. SP1 34 D5
Scots La. SP1 34 D6
Senior Dri. SP2 37 E4

Seth Ward Dri. SP1 35 F4
Shady Bower. SP1 37 F1
Shady Bower Clo. SP1 37 F1
*Shakespeare Pl,
Windsor St. SP2 34 C6
Shakespeare Rd. SP1 34 C3
*Sharrat Av,
Ash Cres. SP1 35 F2
Sheen Clo. SP2 33 D2
Shelley Dri. SP1 34 C3
Shropshire Clo. SP2 33 D2
Sidney St. SP2 34 C6
Silver St. SP1 36 D1
Silverwood Dri. SP1 35 H5
Skew Bridge Rd. SP1 34 A5
Skew Rd. SP2 33 C5
Smeaton Rd. SP2 36 B1
Somerset Rd. SP1 35 E4
South St. SP2 36 D1
South Western Rd. SP2 34 C6
Southampton Rd. SP1 37 E2
*Spring Ct,
Windsor Rd. SP1 34 C6
Stanley Little Rd. SP2 33 C4
Station Ter. SP2 34 C6
Stephens Clo. SP2 36 B2
Stephenson Rd. SP2 34 B6
Stockwood Clo. SP1 35 F4
Stratford Ct. SP1 34 D4
Stratford Rd. SP1 34 B1
Suffolk Rd. SP2 36 B3
Summerlock App. SP2 34 D6
Sunnyhill Rd. SP1 35 E3
Sussex Rd. SP2 36 B3
Swallow Mead. SP2 36 D4
Swan Clo. SP2 36 D3
Swaynes Clo. SP1 35 E5
Swift Down. SP2 36 D4
Sycamore Dri. SP1 35 F2
Syringa Ct. SP2 34 A6

Talbot Clo. SP1 35 F3
Telford Rd. SP1 36 B1
The Avenue, Fugglestone
St Peter. SP2 33 A3
The Avenue,
Laverstock. SP1 35 G6
The Avenue,
Salisbury. SP1 37 F1
The Beeches. SP1 37 F2
The Brambles. SP1 35 F5
The Crusades. SP1 35 F3
The Crescent. SP1 37 E1
The Friary. SP1 37 F2
The Green. SP1 35 G5
The Hardings. SP2 34 C6
The Maples. SP2 34 C5
The Meadows. SP1 37 G1
The Oak Bournes. SP1 34 F2
The Orchard. SP1 35 F5
The Steadings. SP4 35 G1
The Valley. SP2 33 D2
The Ventry. SP1 35 E5
Thistlebarrow Rd. SP1 34 D3
Thompson Clo. SP2 36 C5
Tollgate Rd. SP1 37 E1
Tournament Rd. SP2 34 A4
Tower Mews. SP1 35 E5
Town Path. SP2 36 C2
Trinity St. SP1 37 E1
Tryhorn Dri. SP1 35 F2
Turner Clo. SP2 36 B2
Tylers Clo. SP2 36 B2

Upper St. SP2 36 B2

Vanessa Av. SP1 35 G6
Verona Rd. SP1 34 C3
Victoria Ct. SP1 34 D4
Victoria Rd. SP1 34 D5

Wain-a-long Rd. SP1 · 35 F6
Warwick Clo. SP1 34 D4
Waterloo Rd. SP1 37 F2
Waters Rd. SP1 34 D3
Watersmeet Rd. SP2 36 D3
Watt Rd. SP2 36 B1
Wavel Rd. SP2 36 D3
Wellington Way. SP2 34 A4
Wessex Rd. SP1 35 F6
West End Rd. SP2 34 B5
West St. SP2 34 C6
West Walk. SP1 36 D2
Westbourne Clo. SP1 37 F1
Western Way. SP2 33 C4
Westfield Clo. SP1 35 G5
Westminster Rd. SP2 34 C5
*Westwood Rd. SP2 33 C3

Whitbread Rd. SP2 33 D2
Whitebridge Rd. SP1 35 G6
Whitefriars Way. SP1 37 E2
William Clo. SP1 35 G6
Willow Clo. SP1 35 G5
Wilman Way. SP2 36 C5
Wilton Rd. SP2 34 A5
Wiltshire Rd. SP2 36 B3
Winchester St. SP1 35 E6
Winding Way. SP2 33 D4
Windlesham Rd. SP1 35 E3
Windsor Rd. SP2 34 C6
Windsor St. SP2 34 C6
Wolferston Dri. SP1 35 G2
Woodbury Gdns. SP2 37 E4
Woodford Rd. SP2 34 A1
Woodland Way. SP1 35 G5
Woodside Rd. SP2 33 D4
Woodstock Rd. SP1 35 E5
Woodville Rd. SP1 35 F3
Wordsworth Rd. SP1 35 E5
Wrenscroft. SP2 36 D5
Wyndham Rd. SP1 34 D5
Wyndham Ter. SP1 35 E5

York Rd. SP2 34 C6

SWINDON

Abbey View Rd. SN2 39 E3
Abington Way. SN2 40 B2
Abney Moor. SN3 45 G5
Acacia Gro. SN2 39 H4
Acorn Clo. SN3 45 E3
Addison Cres. SN2 40 C3
Adwalton Clo. SN5 42 B4
Affleck Clo. SN5 42 C3
Ainsworth Rd. SN3 44 D4
Akenfield Clo. SN2 39 F2
Akers Way. SN2 38 D4
Alanbrooke Cres. SN2 39 F5
Alba Clo. SN5 42 A1
Albert St. SN1 44 A4
Albion St. SN1 43 G3
Aldborough Clo. SN5 42 C1
Aldbourne Clo. SN2 39 H1
Alder Clo. SN2 38 D2
Alexandra Rd. SN1 43 H1
Alfred St. SN1 44 A1
Allington Rd. SN2 39 G1
Allison Ct. SN2 39 F4
Alnwick. SN5 42 C4
Alpine Clo. SN5 42 B1
Alton Clo. SN2 39 H1
Alvescot Rd. SN3 44 B3
Alveston Clo. SN5 42 D2
Amber Ct. SN1 44 B1
Amberley Clo. SN2 39 H3
Ambrose Rd. SN1 44 A5
Amersham Rd. SN3 45 E4
Amesbury Clo. SN2 39 G1
Ancona Clo. SN5 42 B1
Anderson Clo. SN3 45 F4
Andover St. SN1 43 F3
Angelica Clo. SN2 38 D3
Angler Rd. SN5 42 C2
Anglesey Clo. SN5 42 C2
Angus Clo. SN5 42 B1
Anise Clo. SN2 38 D3
Ansty Walk. SN3 39 G1
Applewood Ct. SN5 42 D3
Archers Clo. SN1 40 C1
Argyle St. SN2 40 A5
Arkwright Rd. SN2 40 A1
Arley Clo. SN2 39 F1
Arlington Clo. SN3 45 E1
Arliss Clo. SN3 39 G1
Armstrong St. SN1 44 A1
Arnfield Moor. SN3 45 G5
Arun Rd. SN2 39 F3
Arundel Clo. SN3 44 C4
Ascham Rd. SN5 42 B2
Ash Gdns. SN5 38 B5
Ash Gdns. SN3 41 G3
Ash Gro. SN2 39 H4
Ashburnham Clo. SN5 42 A4
Ashbury Av. SN3 45 E1
Ashford Rd. SN1 43 G3
Ashie Clo. SN5 38 C4
Ashington Way. SN5 42 C4
Ashley Clo. SN3 44 D4
Ashmore Clo. SN3 45 F2
Ashwell Clo. SN3 44 C5
Ashworth Dri. SN5 43 E2
Askerton Clo. SN5 38 A6
Askew Clo. SN5 42 A3

Atbara Clo. SN2 39 F3
Athena Av. SN2 40 B5
Attlee Cres. SN2 40 C3
Atworth Clo. SN2 39 G1
Auden Clo. SN2 39 E1
Audley Clo. SN5 42 A4
Austen Cres. SN3 45 F3
Avebury Rd. SN2 39 G2
Avening St. SN2 40 A6
Avens Clo. SN2 38 D2
Avenue Rd. SN1 44 A4
Avocet Clo. SN3 40 D2
Avonmead. SN2 39 E3
Axbridge Clo. SN3 44 D3
Aylesbury St. SN1 43 H1
Aymer Pl. SN3 45 E3
Ayrshire Clo. SN5 42 B1
Azelin Ct. SN3 41 E4

Babington Pk. SN5 42 A3
Bainbridge Clo. SN3 42 B3
Baird Clo. SN5 38 B6
Bakers Ct. SN3 41 E4
Bale Clo. SN5 42 A3
Balmoral Clo. SN3 44 D5
Banbury Clo. SN3 44 C4
Bancroft Clo. SN2 42 A2
Bankfoot Clo. SN5 42 C1
Bankside. SN1 43 F4
Banwell Av. SN3 44 D3
Barbury Clo. SN2 39 E3
Barn Moor Clo. SN3 45 G4
Barnard Clo. SN3 45 E1
Barnfield Clo. SN2 43 E1
Barnfield Rd. SN2 43 E1
Barnstable Clo. SN3 44 D3
Barnstead Clo. SN5 42 B4
Barnum Ct. SN2 43 F1
Baron Clo. SN3 41 E3
Barrington Clo. SN3 45 G5
Barrowby Gate. SN3 40 D3
Barry Glen Clo. SN2 40 C5
Barton Rd. SN2 39 E3
Basil Clo. SN2 38 D3
Basingstoke Clo. SN5 42 B4
Baskerville Rd. SN3 45 G1
Bath Rd. SN1 43 H4
Bathampton St. SN1 43 G2
Bathurst Rd. SN1 44 A1
Baxter Clo. SN2 39 F1
Baydon Clo. SN2 39 E3
Bayleaf Av. SN2 38 D2
Beales Clo. SN1 43 H1
Beatrice St. SN2 39 H6
Beauchamp Clo. SN2 39 E3
Beaufort Grn. SN3 45 E3
Beaulieu Clo. SN5 42 D4
Beaumaris Rd. SN5 42 C3
Beaumont Rd. SN3 44 C2
Beckhampton St. SN1 44 A2
Beddington Ct. SN3 40 D2
Bedford Rd. SN3 44 C2
Bedwyn Clo. SN2 40 A4
Beech Av. SN2 39 F4
Beech Dri. SN5 38 B4
Beechcroft Rd. SN2 40 B3
Beehive Clo. SN5 38 A6
Belgrave St. SN1 44 A3
Bell Gdns. SN3 41 G3
Belle Vue Rd. SN1 44 A3
Bellver. SN5 42 C3
Belmont Clo. SN2 40 D3
Belmont Cres. SN1 43 G5
Belsay. SN5 42 C4
Belvedere Rd. SN3 44 D4
Bembridge Clo. SN3 45 E3
Bentley Clo. SN3 44 D2
Benwell Clo. SN2 42 C2
Berenger Clo. SN1 44 B4
Beresford Clo. SN3 45 F4
Bergman Clo. SN2 39 G1
Berkeley Lawns. SN3 44 C5
Berkshire Dri. SN5 42 D4
Berrington Rd. SN3 44 D4
Berry Copse. SN3 38 A5
Bess Rd. SN5 42 A4
Bessemer Clo. SN2 39 F5
Bessemer Rd East. SN2 39 F5
Bessemer Rd West.
SN2 39 F5
Betony Clo. SN2 39 F5
Bevan Clo. SN2 40 C4
Beverley. SN5 42 C4
Beverstone Gro. SN3 44 C4
Bevil. SN5 42 B4
Bevisland. SN3 45 E4
Bibury Rd. SN3 44 B3

Bicton Rd. SN2 39 F1
Bideford Clo. SN3 44 D3
Bindon Clo. SN5 42 A3
Birch St. SN1 43 F4
Birchwood Rd. SN3 41 E5
Birdbrook Rd. SN2 40 C2
Birdcombe Rd. SN5 42 C2
Bishopdale Clo. SN5 38 B6
Bisley Clo. SN3 44 D3
Bittern Rd. SN3 45 G2
Blackmore Clo. SN3 45 G1
Blackstone Av. SN3 45 F3
Blackthorn La. SN2 39 G3
Blake Cres. SN3 41 E4
Blakeney Av. SN3 45 E1
Blakesley Clo. SN3 44 D4
Blandford Clo. SN3 45 E2
Bletchley Clo. SN3 45 F4
Blockley Rise. SN3 40 D2
Bloomsbury Clo. SN5 42 B3
Blunsdon Rd. SN2 39 E1
Bodiam Dri. SN3 42 D3
Bodiam Dri North. SN5 42 D3
Bodiam Dri South. SN5 42 D4
Bodmin Clo. SN3 44 D2
Boldrewood. SN3 45 F4
Boleyn Clo. SN5 42 A2
Bolingbroke Rd. SN2 39 E4
Bonner Clo. SN5 42 A2
Borage Clo. SN2 38 D2
Boscombe Rd. SN3 39 E3
Bosham Clo. SN5 42 C3
Bosworth Rd. SN5 42 B2
Bothwell Rd. SN3 44 C1
Botley Copse. SN5 38 B4
Boundary Clo. SN2 40 C1
Bourne Rd. SN2 39 E4
Bourton Av. SN3 41 E5
Bouverie Av. SN3 44 B4
Bowleymead. SN3 45 F2
Bowling Green La. SN1 44 A5
Bowman Clo. SN3 41 E4
Bowood Rd. SN1 43 G4
Boydell Clo. SN5 38 B6
Bradenham Rd. SN5 42 A3
Bradford Rd. SN1 44 A4
Bradley Rd. SN2 40 B3
Bradwell Moor. SN3 45 G5
Braemar Clo. SN3 44 D5
Bramble Clo. SN2 40 B5
Bramble Dri. SN2 40 C5
Bramdean Clo. SN2 39 F1
Bramwell Clo. SN2 40 C1
Brandon Clo. SN3 42 B3
Branksome Rd. SN2 39 E3
Bratton Clo. SN2 39 G2
Braybrooke Clo. SN5 38 A6
Brecon Clo. SN3 44 C5
Brem Hill Clo. SN2 39 H2
Brendon Walk. SN3 45 E2
Briar Fields. SN1 44 B1
Bridge End Rd. SN3 40 C6
Bridge St. SN1 43 G2
Bridgeman Clo. SN3 41 E4
Bridgemead Clo. SN5 42 D1
Bridgewater Clo. SN2 43 F1
Bridport Rd. SN3 40 D3
Briery Clo. SN3 40 D3
Bright St. SN2 40 B6
Brind Clo. SN3 45 G2
Brindley Clo. SN2 39 E6
Brington Rd. SN3 41 E6
Bristol St. SN1 43 G2
Britannia Pl. SN1 44 A4
Brixham Av. SN3 44 C5
Broad St. SN1 44 A4
Broadmead Walk. SN3 45 E1
Broadway. SN2 39 F3
Bromley Clo. SN3 44 C2
Bronte Clo. SN3 45 F4
Brook Lime Clo. SN2 38 D2
Brookdene. SN2 39 E2
Brooklands Av. SN3 39 F5
Brooks Clo. SN2 40 B2
Brooksby Way. SN3 44 C5
Broome Manor La. SN3 44 C5
Browning Clo. SN3 41 E3
Bruce St. SN2 43 F1
Bruddel Gro. SN3 44 B5
Brunswick St. SN1 44 A4
Bryanston Way. SN3 45 E2
Bryony Way. SN2 38 D2
Buckhurst Cres. SN3 44 D4
Buckingham Rd. SN3 44 B5
Buckland Clo. SN3 44 D2
Bucklebury Clo. SN3 40 D5
Buckthorn Dri. SN2 38 D3
Buie Clo. SN5 38 C4

Buller St. SN2 40 B6
Bullfinch Clo. SN3 45 G2
Bunce Rd. SN3 40 D5
Burbage Rd. SN2 39 H1
Burden Clo. SN3 41 E5
Burford Av. SN3 44 B3
Burgess Clo. SN3 40 D5
Burghley Clo. SN3 44 D2
Burnet Clo. SN2 38 D2
Burnham Clo. SN3 44 D2
Burns Way. SN2 40 C3
Buttermere. SN3 45 G4
Butterworth St. SN1 43 F2
Byfield Way. SN3 41 E6
Byrd Clo. SN5 42 A3
Byron Ct. SN3 41 G2
Byron St. SN1 44 A3

Cabot Dri. SN5 42 A2
Cadley Clo. SN3 40 A4
Caernarvon Walk. SN3 44 C5
Cagney Dri. SN2 39 F1
Cairndow Way. SN2 40 B2
Calder Clo. SN2 39 F2
Callaghan Clo. SN3 40 D4
Callenders. SN5 43 E2
Calvert Rd. SN3 44 B2
Cambria Bri Rd. SN1 43 G2
Cambria Pl. SN1 43 G3
Cambridge Clo. SN3 44 C4
Camden Clo. SN5 42 A3
Cameron Clo. SN3 40 D5
Campden Rd. SN3 44 B3
Campion Gate. SN5 42 A2
Camton Rd. SN5 42 A1
Canal Walk. SN1 43 G2
Canford Clo. SN3 45 E2
Cannon St. SN1 44 A3
Canterbury Clo. SN3 44 C5
Capesthorne Dri. SN2 39 E1
Capitol Clo. SN3 41 F6
Caprice Clo. SN5 42 A1
Cardigan Clo. SN3 44 C4
Cardwell Clo. SN3 45 E1
Carey Clo. SN5 42 B3
Carfax St. SN1 43 H1
Carlisle Av. SN3 44 B6
Carlton Gate. SN3 44 D6
Carman Clo. SN3 41 E4
Carpenters La. SN2 40 B6
Carr St. SN1 43 G2
Carraway Dri. SN2 38 C3
Carroll Clo. SN3 45 F4
Carronbridge Rd. SN5 42 C2
Carshalton Rd. SN3 45 E4
Carslake Clo. SN3 45 E3
Carstairs Av. SN3 44 D4
Cartwright Dri. SN5 38 B6
Casson Rd. SN3 40 D4
Castilian Mews. SN5 42 B1
Castle Dore. SN5 42 B3
Castlefield Clo. SN5 42 C2
Castleton Rd. SN5 42 A1
Castleview Rd. SN3 41 F5
Catherine St. SN1 43 G2
Catherine Wayte Clo. SN2 39 F3
Catmint Clo. SN2 38 D3
Caulfield Rd. SN3 40 A6
Cavendish Sq. SN3 44 D4
Caversham Clo. SN3 44 C3
Cavie Clo. SN5 38 A6
Caxton Clo. SN3 44 C3
Cayenne Pk. SN3 38 C3
Cecil Rd. SN3 44 D2
Cedars Clo. SN2 39 F4
Centurion Way. SN3 41 F6
Chadworth Gate. SN3 44 C6
Chalford Av. SN3 45 E1
Chamberlain Rd. SN3 40 D4
Chancellor Clo. SN5 42 A2
Chandler Clo. SN1 44 B3
Chandos Clo. SN5 42 B2
Chantry Rd. SN2 39 E4
Chapel Rd. SN3 41 G2
Chapel St. SN2 40 B6
Charfield Clo. SN3 44 D4
Charlbury Clo. SN2 39 E3
Charles McPherson Gdns. SN3 45 F3
Charlotte Mews. SN1 44 B4
Charlton Clo. SN2 40 A2
Charminster Clo. SN2 45 E2
Charolais Dri. SN5 42 B1
Chartley Grn. SN5 42 A3
Chase Wood. SN5 38 A5
Chatsworth Rd. SN2 39 F2
Cheddar Rd. SN2 39 E3

Chelmsford Rd. SN5 42 C1
Cheltenham St. SN1 43 G1
Chelworth Rd. SN2 39 E3
Cheney Manor Rd. SN2 39 F4
Chepstow Clo. SN5 42 C4
Cheraton Clo. SN3 45 E1
Cherhill Ct. SN2 39 E3
Cherry Tree Gro. SN3 39 H4
Chervil Rd. SN2 38 D2
Chesford Clo. SN3 44 D5
Chester St. SN1 43 G2
Chesterfield Clo. SN5 42 C2
Chestnut Av. SN2 40 A4
Chevalier Clo. SN5 42 A1
Cheviot Clo. SN5 42 B2
Chickerell Rd. SN3 44 D2
Chicory Clo. SN2 38 C3
Chilton Gdns. SN3 39 E4
Chilworth Clo. SN2 39 E1
Chippenham Clo. SN2 39 G1
Chippenham Way. SN2 39 G1
Chives Way. SN2 38 D3
Chobham Clo. SN3 40 D2
Christie Clo. SN3 45 F4
Chudleigh. SN5 42 B4
Church Grnd. SN3 41 H2
Church Pl. SN1 43 F2
Church St. SN3 41 E4
Church Walk. SN1 43 G3
Church Walk Nth. SN2 39 F3
Church Walk Sth. SN2 39 F4
Church Way. SN3 40 D5
Churchfield. SN2 39 E2
Churchward Av. SN2 39 F5
Cirencester Way. SN2 40 B6
Clanfield Rd. SN3 45 E3
Clare Walk. SN5 42 C3
Clarence St. SN1 44 A2
Clarendon La. SN1 43 F3
Clarke Dri. SN5 38 B6
Clary Rd. SN2 38 D2
Clayhill Copse. SN5 38 A5
Clays Clo. SN2 40 B3
Cleasby Clo. SN5 42 D2
Cleeve Lawns. SN1 44 C5
Clevedon Clo. SN3 44 D2
Cleves Clo. SN2 42 B2
Clifton Rd. SN1 43 G3
Clinton Clo. SN5 42 A3
Cloche Way. SN2 40 C4
Cloudberry Rd. SN2 39 E1
Clouts Wood. SN5 38 B4
Clover Lands. SN2 38 D2
Clover Pk. SN2 38 D3
Clydesdale Clo. SN5 42 B1
Cobden Rd. SN3 39 F6
Colbert Pk. SN2 39 F1
Colbourne St. SN1 44 B1
Colchester Clo. SN5 42 D4
Cole Clo. SN3 45 F2
Colebrook Rd. SN3 41 E6
Coleridge Rd. SN2 39 E1
College St. SN1 43 H2
Collett Av. SN2 39 F5
Collingsmead. SN3 45 F3
Collins La. SN3 38 A2
Coln Cres. SN3 39 F2
Colston Clo. SN3 44 D3
Comfrey Clo. SN2 38 D3
Commercial Rd. SN1 43 G2
Commonweal Rd. SN1 43 G4
Compton Clo. SN3 45 E4
Conan Doyle Walk. SN3 45 G4
Conisborough. SN5 42 C3
Conrad Clo. SN3 45 F4
Constable Rd. SN3 40 C4
Constantine Clo. SN3 41 F6
Conway Rd. SN3 45 F4
Conyers Clo. SN5 42 A3
Coombe Rd. SN3 39 E3
Cooper Fld. SN2 39 F1
Coppice Clo. SN3 38 D3
Copse Av. SN1 40 C6
Corby Av. SN3 44 B5
Corfe Clo. SN2 39 F3
Corfe Rd. SN5 42 C3
Coriander Way. SN2 38 D2
Corinium Way. SN3 41 F6
Cornflower Rd. SN2 38 D2
Cornmarsh Way. SN3 45 G1
Cornwall Rd. SN2 39 G5
Corporation St. SN1 44 A1
Corral Clo. SN5 38 B6
Corsham Rd. SN2 39 H2
Corton Cres. SN3 44 C2
Cottars Clo. SN3 41 E3
Cottington Clo. SN5 42 B4
County Rd. SN1 44 B1

Courtenay Rd. SN3 44 D2
Courts Knapp Ct. SN1 43 F3
Covingham Dri. SN3 41 F6
Cowdrey Clo. SN5 42 C4
Cowleaze Walk. SN2 40 C3
Crabtree Copse. SN5 38 B5
Crampton Rd. SN3 44 D1
Cranmore Av. SN3 44 D4
Crawford Clo. SN5 42 B4
Crawley Av. SN3 41 E5
Cricklade Rd. SN2 40 A1
Cricklade St. SN1 44 B3
Crieff Clo. SN3 45 E2
Crispin Clo. SN3 41 E3
Croft Rd. SN1 44 A6
Crombey St. SN1 43 G2
Crompton Rd. SN2 40 A1
Cromwell. SN5 42 B4
Cross St. SN1 44 A3
Crossways Av. SN2 39 H3
Crosswood Rd. SN3 44 D2
Crudwell Way. SN2 39 H1
Cuckoos Mead. SN3 45 G1
Cullerne Rd. SN3 41 F5
Cumberland Rd. SN3 44 B2
Cunetio Rd. SN3 41 F6
Cunningham Rd. SN2 39 G4
Curtis St. SN1 43 G3
Cypress Gro. SN2 39 G4

Dacre Rd. SN3 44 D2
Daisy Clo. SN2 38 D3
Dalefoot Clo. SN5 38 A5
Dallas Av. SN3 45 E1
Dalton Clo. SN3 44 D1
Dalwood Clo. SN3 45 E4
Dammas La. SN1 44 B4
Danestone Clo. SN5 42 A1
Darcey Clo. SN5 42 A2
Darius Way. SN2 39 F1
Darnley Clo. SN3 44 C2
Dart Av. SN2 39 G3
Darwin Clo. SN3 45 E1
Davenham Clo. SN3 44 D4
Davenwood. SN2 40 C2
Dawlish Rd. SN3 45 E2
Day House La. SN3 45 E5
Days Clo. SN3 40 D5
Deacon St. SN1 43 G3
Dean St. SN2 43 F2
Deben Cres. SN2 39 F2
Deburgh St. SN2 43 F2
Deerhurst Way. SN5 42 D3
Delamere Dri. SN3 40 D3
Denbeck Wood. SN5 42 C1
Denbigh Clo. SN3 44 C4
Denholme Rd. SN3 44 D4
Denton Ct. SN3 41 E4
Derby Clo. SN3 39 E5
Derwent Dri. SN2 40 C2
Desborough. SN5 42 B5
Deva Clo. SN3 41 F6
*Devereux Clo,
  Grindal Clo. SN5 42 A3
Devizes Rd. SN1 44 A4
Devon Rd. SN2 39 G5
Dewberry Clo. SN2 39 E2
Dewell Mews. SN3 44 B4
Dexter Clo. SN5 42 B2
Dickens Clo. SN3 45 F4
Dinmore Rd. SN2 39 F1
Dixon St. SN1 43 G3
Dobbin Clo. SN3 45 G1
Dockle Way. SN3 40 C3
Don Clo. SN2 39 F2
Donnington Gro. SN3 44 C1
Dorcan Way. SN3 45 E1
Dorchester Rd. SN1 44 C1
Dores Clo. SN2 40 B3
Dores Rd. SN2 40 B3
Douglas Rd. SN3 44 C2
Dover St. SN1 44 A3
Dovetrees. SN3 45 G1
Dowling St. SN1 43 H3
Downland Rd. SN2 38 D3
Downs View Rd. SN3 44 C6
Downton Rd. SN2 39 G2
Drakes Way. SN3 44 C2
Draycott Clo. SN3 44 D2
Drew St. SN2 43 E1
Drove Rd. SN1 44 B3
Dryden St. SN1 43 G3
Duchess Way. SN2 40 B2
Dudley Rd. SN3 44 D2
Dudmore Rd. SN3 44 B2
Dukes Clo. SN2 40 B2
Dulverton Av. SN3 44 D3
Dunbarton Ter. SN1 44 A3

Dunbeath Rd. SN2 40 B5
Dunraven Clo. SN3 44 C4
Dunsford Clo. SN1 43 F3
Dunster Clo. SN3 44 C5
Dunwich Dri. SN5 42 D3
Durham St. SN1 44 A3
Durnford Rd. SN2 40 A2
Durrington Walk. SN2 39 H2

Eagle Clo. SN3 45 G1
Earl Clo. SN5 42 A1
Eastcott Hill. SN1 43 H3
Eastcott Rd. SN1 43 H3
Eastern Av. SN3 44 B2
Eastleaze Rd. SN5 42 C2
Eastmere. SN3 45 G4
Eastville Rd. SN2 39 H3
Eaton Clo. SN3 44 D4
Eaton Wood. SN5 38 A5
Eccleston Clo. SN3 45 E4
Ecklington. SN3 45 E3
Edale Moor. SN3 45 G1
Edgehill. SN5 42 B4
Edgeware Rd. SN1 43 H2
Edgeworth Clo. SN5 42 C1
Edinburgh St. SN2 40 A5
Edington Clo. SN5 42 D3
Edison Rd. SN3 44 A3
Edmund St. SN1 44 A3
Egerton Clo. SN3 45 E1
Elborough Rd. SN3 38 D3
Eldene Dri. SN3 45 E3
Elder Clo. SN2 38 D3
Elgin Dri. SN2 40 B5
Eliot Clo. SN3 45 G4
Elm Gro. SN5 38 B6
Elm Rd. SN2 39 F4
Elmina Rd. SN1 44 A1
Elmore. SN3 45 E4
Elmswood Clo. SN2 40 B2
Elsham Way. SN2 39 F2
Elsie Hazel Ct. SN5 42 B4
Elstree Way. SN2 39 F1
Ely Clo. SN5 42 D3
Emlyn Sq. SN1 43 G2
Emmanuel Clo. SN2 39 F2
Enford Av. SN2 39 H1
Eric Long Clo. SN3 45 F3
Erlestoke Way. SN2 39 H1
Ermin St. SN3 40 C2
Espringham Pl. SN2 40 B2
Essex Walk. SN3 44 A2
Euclid St. SN1 44 A2
Euro Way. SN5 42 A5
Evelyn St. SN3 44 B5
Everleigh Rd. SN2 39 H2
Eworth Clo. SN5 42 A3
Exbury Clo. SN2 39 F1
Exe Clo. SN2 39 G2
Exeter St. SN1 43 G2
Exmouth St. SN1 43 G3

Fairfax St. SN3 44 C1
Fairford Cres. SN3 39 H1
Fairholme Way. SN2 40 C3
Fairlawn. SN3 45 F5
Fairview. SN1 43 G3
Falconscroft. SN3 45 F1
Falmouth Gro. SN1 44 C1
Fanstones Rd. SN3 45 E4
Faraday Rd. SN3 45 G3
Fareham Clo. SN3 45 E3
Faringdon Rd. SN1 43 G2
Farleigh Cres. SN3 44 C5
Farman Clo. SN3 45 F4
Farnborough Rd. SN3 44 D5
Farnsby St. SN1 43 G2
Farrfield. SN2 40 B3
Farriers Clo. SN1 40 B6
Feather Wood. SN5 38 C2
Fenland Clo. SN5 42 A1
Fennel Clo. SN2 38 D2
Ferndale Rd. SN2 39 F6
Fernham Rd. SN2 39 E4
Ferrers Dri. SN5 42 A2
Field Rise. SN1 43 G5
Fieldfare. SN3 45 F1
Finchdale. SN3 41 F6
Fir Tree Clo. SN2 39 F4
Firecrest Vw. SN3 45 G2
Firth Clo. SN2 39 F3
Fitzmaurice Clo. SN3 45 F1
Fitzroy Rd. SN1 44 A5
Fleet St. SN1 43 G2
Fleetwood Ct. SN5 42 B4
Fleming Way. SN1 43 H2

Flint Hill. SN5 4
Florence St. SN2 3
Folkestone Rd. SN1 4
Fonthill Walk. SN3 4
Ford St. SN1 4
Forester Clo. SN3 4
Forsley Clo. SN3 4
Forum Clo. SN3 4
Fosse Clo. SN2 4
Fowey. SN5 4
Fox Hill Clo. SN2 3
Foxbridge. SN3 4
Foxglove Rd. SN2 38
Foxley Clo. SN2 40
Foxwood. SN5 42
Frampton Clo. SN5 42
Francomes. SN2 39
Frankland Rd. SN1 42
Frankton Gdns. SN3 41
Fraser Clo. SN3 45
Freshbrook Way. SN5 42
Friesian Clo. SN5 42
Friesland Clo. SN5 42
Frilford Dri. SN3 40
Frith Copse. SN5 38
Frobisher Dri. SN3 44
Frome Rd. SN2 39
Fry Clo. SN5 43
Fullers Clo. SN2 40
Furlong Clo. SN2 39
Furze Clo. SN5 38
Fyfield Av. SN2 39
Fyne Clo. SN5 38

Gainsborough Way. SN5 42
Gairlock Clo. SN5 38
Galloway Clo. SN5 42
Galsworthy Clo. SN3 45
Gambia St. SN1 44
Gantlett Dene. SN3 45
Ganton Clo. SN2 40
Ganton Way. SN2 40
Garfield Clo. SN3 45
Garrard Way. SN3 40
Garson Rd. SN2 39
Gartons Rd. SN5 42
Gaynor Clo. SN2 39
Gays Pl. SN2 40
Gayton Way. SN3 41
George St. SN1 43
Gerard Walk. SN5 42
Gibbs Clo. SN3 45
Gifford Rd. SN3 41
Gilberts Hill. SN1 43
Gilling Way. SN5 45
Gipsy La. SN2 40
Gladstone St. SN1 44
Glenwood Clo. SN1 44
Glevum Rd. SN3 41
Globe St. SN1 43
Gloucester St. SN1 43
Goddard Av. SN1 43
Godolphin Clo. SN5 42
Godwin Rd. SN3 41
Goldcrest Walk. SN3 45
Goldsborough Clo. SN5 42
Gooch St. SN1 44
Gordon Gdns. SN1 43
Gordon Rd. SN1 44
Goulding Av. SN3 40
Gower Clo. SN5 42
Gower Clo. SN2 40
Grafton Rd. SN2 40
Graham St. SN1 44
Grailey Clo. SN3 45
Granary Clo. SN5 38
Grandison Clo. SN5 42
Grange Dri. SN3 40
Grange Park Way. SN5 42
Grantham Clo. SN3 42
Grantley Clo. SN3 44
Granville St. SN1 43
Grasmere. SN3 45
Graythwaite Clo. SN2 39
Great Western Way. SN5 42
Green Hill Rd. SN2 39
Green Meadow Av. SN3 39
Green Rd. SN2 40
Green Valley Av. SN2 39
Greenbridge Rd. SN3 44
Greenfields. SN3 41
Greenlands Rd. SN2 40
Greenway Clo. SN3 45
Greenwich Clo. SN2 39
Gresham Clo. SN3 44
Greywethers Av. SN3 44

ths Clo. SN3 41 E5
dal Dri. SN5 42 A3
mont Dri. SN5 42 B3
venor Rd. SN1 43 F4
ndwell Rd. SN1 44 A2
elands Av. SN1 44 A5
es St. SN2 43 F2
dys. SN3 45 F4
dford Av. SN3 44 C5
py St. SN2 43 F2

kett Clo. SN2 40 B2
kleton Rise. SN3 41 E6
don Clo. SN5 42 A3
leigh Clo. SN5 42 D2
leigh Rise. SN3 40 D2
rians Clo. SN3 41 F6
g Clo. SN2 40 B3
am Moor. SN3 45 G5
ble Rd. SN3 39 F3
ilton Clo. SN3 44 C1
npshire Clo. SN5 42 B1
npton Dri. SN5 42 A2
nworthy Rd. SN3 45 F2
bury Rd. SN3 44 D4
ndel St. SN2 39 H6
nnington Clo. SN2 39 G1
nson Clo. SN5 42 B1
bour Clo. SN2 39 F3
court Rd. SN2 39 F6
die Clo. SN3 40 D5
rding St. SN1 43 G2
rdwick Clo. SN2 39 F2
re Clo. SN2 40 C1
ebell Clo. SN2 39 E2
rgreaves Rd. SN2 40 B1
rlech Clo. SN5 42 C4
rlestone Rd. SN3 41 E6
rptree Clo. SN5 38 A6
rrington Walk. SN3 44 D1
rris Rd. SN3 39 F5
rrow Clo. SN3 40 D5
rtland Clo. SN3 44 D1
rtsthorn Clo. SN3 38 D3
rvester Clo. SN5 38 A6
rvey Gro. SN2 39 F5
slemere Clo. SN3 45 E4
atfield Clo. SN2 39 E1
athaway Rd. SN2 40 B2
atherall Clo. SN3 41 F5
atherley Rd. SN3 44 B1
athersage Moor. SN3 45 G5
atton Gro. SN3 44 C2
avelock St. SN1 43 H2
aven Clo. SN3 41 E6
awker Rd. SN3 45 E3
awkfinch Clo. SN5 45 G2
awkins St. SN2 43 F1
awkswood. SN3 41 F6
awksworth Way. SN2 43 G1
awthorn Av. SN2 39 H4
ay La. SN4 42 A6
aydon Ct. SN2 39 E2
aydon Court Dri. SN2 39 E2
aydon End La. SN2 39 E1
aydon St. SN1 43 H1
aydon View Rd. SN2 39 H3
aydonleigh Dri. SN2 39 E2
aynes Clo. SN5 45 E4
ayward Clo. SN2 39 G1
azebury Cres. SN3 45 F1
azel Gro. SN2 39 H3
eadlands Gro. SN2 40 B4
eath Way. SN3 41 E6
eathcote Clo. SN5 38 B6
eaton Clo. SN2 39 F1
eddington Clo. SN2 39 H2
edgerow Clo. SN3 45 E3
edges Clo. SN3 41 E4
elmsdale. SN2 39 E3
elston Rd. SN3 44 D3
enley Rd. SN3 44 D4
enry St. SN1 43 G2
epworth Rd. SN2 39 F1
ereford Lawns. SN3 44 C5
ermitage La. SN2 40 B3
eronbridge Clo. SN5 42 C2
eronscroft. SN5 45 F1
ertford Clo. SN3 44 C2
esketh Cres. SN3 44 A5
ewitt Clo. SN3 45 F4
exham Clo. SN5 42 B3
eytesbury Gdns. SN5 42 A4
eywood Clo. SN3 39 G2
High St. SN2 39 E2
High St. SN1 44 B4
Highclere Av. SN3 44 C4
Highland Clo. SN5 42 B1

Highmoor Copse. SN5 38 A5
Highnam Clo. SN2 40 D5
Highwood Clo. SN2 38 D3
Highworth Rd. SN3 40 D3
Hill View Rd. SN3 41 F6
Hillary Clo. SN1 39 H3
Hillcrest Clo. SN1 43 G4
Hillingdon Rd. SN3 45 E4
Hillmead Dri. SN5 38 B6
Hillside Av. SN1 43 G4
Hillyard Clo. SN5 42 A3
Hilmarton Av. SN2 39 H1
Hinton St. SN2 40 B6
Hobley Dri. SN3 40 D4
Hodds Hill. SN5 38 B4
Holbein Field. SN5 42 B3
Holbein Mews. SN5 42 B3
Holbein Pl. SN5 42 B3
Holbein Walk. SN5 42 B3
Holbrook Way. SN1 43 G2
Holden Cres. SN2 39 G1
Holliday Clo. SN2 39 F1
Holinshed Pl. SN5 42 B3
Hollins Moor. SN5 45 G5
Holly Clo. SN2 39 F4
Holmleigh. SN2 39 E3
Honeylight Vw. SN2 39 F1
Honeysuckle Clo. SN2 38 D2
Honiton Rd. SN3 45 E3
Hook St. SN5 42 A4
Hoopers Pl. SN1 44 B4
Hopton Clo. SN5 42 C4
Horace St. SN1 43 F2
Horcott Rd. SN5 38 B4
Hornsey Gdns. SN3 40 D2
Horsham Cres. SN3 44 D3
Horseshoe Clo. SN5 38 A5
Horton Rd. SN2 40 C1
Howard Clo. SN3 44 C2
Hughes St. SN2 43 E1
Hungerford Clo. SN5 42 A1
Hunsdon Clo. SN3 44 D2
Hunt St. SN1 44 A3
Hunters Gro. SN3 39 G5
Huntley Clo. SN3 44 C1
Hunts Rise. SN3 41 E1
Hurst Cres. SN3 39 H4
Hyde Rd. SN2 40 B1
Hylder Clo. SN3 38 D3
Hysopp Clo. SN2 38 C2
Hythe Rd. SN1 43 H3

Icomb Clo. SN5 42 C4
Idovers Dri. SN5 42 C3
Iffley Rd. SN2 39 F6
Imber Walk. SN2 39 G1

INDUSTRIAL ESTATES:
Blagrove Employment
 Area. SN5 42 A5
Britannia
 Trade Pk. SN3 40 C4
Cheney Manor
 Ind Est. SN2 39 E5
Churchward Pk. SN5 43 E3
Deloro Ind Est. SN3 40 D4
Delta Business Pk.
 SN5 42 D2
Dorcan Ind Est. SN3 45 G3
Elgin Ind Est. SN2 40 B5
Europa Pk Employment
 Area. SN3 40 D4
Greenbridge
 Ind Est. SN3 40 D6
Groundwell
 Ind Est. SN2 40 B1
Hawksworth
 Ind Est. SN3 43 F1
Headlands
 Ind Est. SN2 40 B4
Hillmead Employment
 Area. SN5 38 B6
Honda Car Plant. SN3 41 E2
Kembrey
 Business Pk. SN2 40 B5
Kendrick Ind Est. SN2 39 E6
Mannington Employment
 Area. SN5 43 E3
Marshgate
 Ind Est. SN1 40 C6
Okus Ind Est. SN1 43 G4
Stratton Road
 Techno
 Trading Est. SN2 40 C5
Thornhill Ind Est.
 SN3 41 G3
Transfer Bridge
 Ind Est. SN2 40 B6

Westmead
 Ind Est. SN5 42 D1
Windmill Hill
 Business Pk. SN5 42 A4
Inglesham Rd. SN2 39 H2
Ipswich St. SN2 39 H6
Irston Way. SN5 42 B4
Isis Clo. SN2 39 G3
Islandsmead. SN3 45 F3
Islington St. SN1 43 H2
Ixworth Clo. SN5 42 B1

*Jack Thorne Clo,
 Linden Way. SN5 38 B4
Jacobs Walk. SN3 45 G3
James Watt Clo. SN2 43 F1
Jasmine Clo. SN2 38 D3
Jefferies Av. SN2 40 B4
Jennings St. SN2 43 F2
Jersey Pk. SN5 42 B1
Jewel Clo. SN5 42 A3
John Herring Cres.
 SN3 40 D5
John St. SN1 43 H2
Jole Clo. SN2 40 C2
Jolliffe St. SN1 43 F2
Joseph St. SN1 43 G3
Jubilee Clo. SN2 38 D4
Juliana Clo. SN5 42 B1
Juniper Clo. SN3 41 E6

Keats Cres. SN2 40 C3
Keble Clo. SN3 45 E1
Kelham Clo. SN3 44 C4
Kelly Gdns. SN2 39 F1
Kelmscot Rd. SN2 39 H3
Kelvin Rd. SN3 44 D1
Kemble Dri. SN2 43 F1
Kembrey St. SN2 40 A5
Kendal. SN5 42 A4
Kenilworth Lawns. SN3 44 C5
Kennedy Dri. SN3 45 F4
Kennet Av. SN2 39 G3
Kent Rd. SN1 43 G3
Kenton Clo. SN3 45 E2
Kenwin Clo. SN3 41 E4
Kerry Clo. SN5 42 B2
Kershaw Rd. SN3 45 F4
Kestrel Dri. SN3 45 G2
Keycroft Copse. SN5 38 A5
Keyneston Rd. SN3 45 F2
Keynsham Walk. SN3 45 E4
Kilben Clo. SN5 42 A1
Kiln La. SN2 39 F5
Kilsby Way. SN3 41 E6
Kilsyth Clo. SN5 42 B3
Kimberley Rd. SN3 44 D4
Kimbolton Clo. SN5 42 B4
Kimmeridge Clo. SN3 45 E2
King Charles Rd. SN5 42 B4
King Henry Dri. SN5 42 A3
King John St. SN1 44 A3
King St. SN1 43 H2
King William St. SN1 44 A3
Kingfisher Dri. SN3 45 F1
Kingscote Clo. SN5 38 A6
Kingsdown Rd. SN2 40 C2
Kingshill Rd. SN1 43 F3
Kingsley Way. SN2 40 A2
Kingsthorpe Gro. SN3 41 F6
Kingston Rd. SN3 44 D4
Kingsway Clo. SN3 44 D3
Kingswood Av. SN3 44 D3
Kipling Gdns. SN2 40 C3
Kirby Clo. SN3 44 C4
Kirkstall Clo. SN5 42 C3
Kirktonhill Rd. SN5 42 D2
Kitchener St. SN2 39 H6
Knapp Clo. SN2 39 H4
Knowsley Rd. SN3 . 44 D4

Laburnum Rd. SN2 39 H4
Lacock Rd. SN2 40 A2
Lady La. SN2 39 E1
Lagos St. SN1 44 A1
Lakeside. SN3 44 B4
Lambert Clo. SN5 42 B4
Lambourne Av. SN3 44 B5
Lamora Clo. SN5 38 A6
Lanac Rd. SN3 40 D6
Langdale Dri. SN5 42 B4
Langford Gro. SN3 44 B2
Langport Clo. SN5 42 B4
Langstone Way. SN5 42 C2
Lanhydrock Clo. SN5 42 B3
Lansbury Dri. SN2 40 C3
Lansdown Rd. SN1 43 H3

Lapwing Clo. SN3 45 G2
Larchmore Clo. SN2 39 G3
Larksfield. SN3 45 F1
Latton Clo. SN2 39 G1
Lawrence Clo. SN3 45 F3
Lawton Clo. SN3 44 C5
Leamington Gro. SN3 44 C5
Leicester St. SN1 44 A2
Leigh Rd. SN2 39 H2
Leighton Av. SN3 44 D4
Lennox Dri. SN3 44 C2
Leslie Clo. SN5 42 B3
Lethbridge Rd. SN1 44 A4
Letterage Rd. SN5 38 B4
Leven. SN5 42 B5
Leverton Gate. SN3 44 C6
Lewisham Clo. SN2 39 E4
Lichen Clo. SN2 38 D3
Liddington St. SN2 40 A4
Liden Dri. SN3 45 F4
Limes Av. SN3 39 G4
Lincoln St. SN1 44 A2
Linden Av. SN2 39 H4
Linden Way. SN5 38 B4
Lineacre Clo. SN5 42 A4
Link Av. SN5 42 C2
Linley Clo. SN1 44 A5
Linnetsdene. SN3 41 F6
Linslade St. SN2 43 F2
Lisle Clo. SN5 42 A3
Little Av. SN2 39 F5
Little London. SN1 44 A3
Littlecote Clo. SN5 42 D3
Locksgreen Cres. SN2 39 E3
Logan Clo. SN3 44 B2
Lomond Clo. SN5 38 C5
London St. SN1 43 G2
Longstock Ct. SN5 42 C2
Longthorpe Clo. SN5 42 D3
Lorne St. SN1 43 G2
Loughborough Clo.
 SN5 42 A3
Louviers Way. SN1 44 A5
Loveage Clo. SN2 38 D3
Lovell Clo. SN3 45 F1
Loveridge Clo. SN2 40 B1
Lowes Clo. SN5 38 C4
Lucerne Clo. SN5 42 A1
Luddesdown Rd. SN5 42 C4
Ludlow Clo. SN3 44 C4
Lulworth Rd. SN2 39 E3
Lumley Clo. SN5 42 A3
Lyddon Way. SN3 39 F3
Lydford Clo. SN5 38 B6
Lyme Way. SN3 39 F2
Lyndhurst Cres. SN3 44 D2
Lyneham Clo. SN2 39 H1
Lynton Rd. SN2 39 E5
Lynwood Gro. SN2 38 D3
Lytchett Way. SN3 45 F2

Martinfield. SN3 45 F1
Masefield Av. SN2 40 B4
Matley Moor. SN3 45 G5
Maxey Clo. SN5 38 B6
Maxwell St. SN1 43 G2
May Clo. SN2 39 H5
Mayfield Clo. SN3 45 E1
Mead Way. SN5 42 C1
Meadow Rd. SN2 43 E1
Meadowcroft. SN2 40 C2
Meadowsweet Clo. SN2 39 E1
Meares Dri. SN3 38 B6
Medgbury Rd. SN1 44 A2
Medina Way. SN2 40 C2
Medway Rd. SN2 39 F3
Melbourne Clo. SN3 44 D5
Melfort Clo. SN5 38 C5
Melford Walk. SN3 45 E1
Melksham Clo. SN2 39 G1
Mellow Ground. SN2 39 E2
Melrose Clo. SN5 42 C1
Melville Clo. SN3 44 C2
Melvyn Webb Pl. SN2 40 B6
Mendip Clo. SN2 39 H3
Menham Clo. SN2 40 A4
Merlin Way. SN3 41 F6
Merrivale Gro. SN1 44 B3
Merton Av. SN2 40 B3
Merton St. SN2 43 H2
Middleleaze Dri. SN5 42 A1
Middleton Clo. SN3 44 C2
Midhurst Av. SN3 45 E2
Midwinter Clo. SN5 38 B5
Midwinter Gdns. SN3 40 D4
Mildenhall Way. SN2 39 G1
Mildmay Clo. SN5 42 A3
Milford St. SN1 43 H2
Mill La. SN1 43 F5
Millbuck Clo. SN2 40 C5
Miller Clo. SN5 42 A1
Milston Av. SN2 39 H2
Milton Rd. SN1 43 G2
Minety Rd. SN2 39 G1
Mint Clo. SN3 38 D3
Monet Clo. SN2 39 F1
Monkton Clo. SN3 45 E4
Monmouth Clo. SN3 44 C4
Montagu St. SN2 43 E1
Monteagle Clo. SN5 42 A3
Montgomery Av. SN2 39 G5
Montrose Clo. SN2 39 E4
Moorhen Clo. SN3 45 G2
Moray Rd. SN2 40 B5
Moredon Pk. SN2 38 D3
Moredon Rd. SN2 39 E3
Moresby Clo. SN5 42 C2
Morie Clo. SN5 38 C5
Morley St. SN1 43 H2
Morris St. SN2 43 E1
Morrison St. SN2 43 E1
Morse St. SN1 43 G3
Mortimer Clo. SN5 42 C1
Mulberry Gro. SN2 39 F4
Mulcaster Av. SN5 42 A3
Mundy Av. SN3 45 E3
Munro Clo. SN3 44 B2
Murdoch Rd. SN3 45 G2
Myrtle Gdns. SN2 39 H4

Nantwich. SN5 42 B5
Napier Clo. SN3 43 F1
Naunton Rd. SN3 44 D2
Nelson St. SN1 43 F3
Ness Clo. SN3 38 C4
Netherton Clo. SN3 45 E4
Nevis Clo. SN5 38 C4
New Bridge Clo. SN1 43 H1
New Bridge Sq. SN1 43 H2
New Meadow Copse.
 SN5 38 B5
Newark Clo. SN5 42 B4
Newburn Cres. SN1 43 F3
Newbury Dri. SN5 42 B4
Newcastle St. SN1 44 A2
Newcombe Dri. SN2 43 F1
Newhall St. SN1 44 H3
Newland Rd. SN2 39 F3
Newport St. SN1 44 A4
Newton Way. SN2 39 H3
Nightingale Rd. SN3 41 H3
Nightwood Copse. SN5 38 B5
Nindum Rd. SN3 41 E5
Norcliffe Rd. SN3 44 D4
Norfolk Clo. SN3 44 D2
Norman Rd. SN2 39 H6
North St. SN1 44 A3
North Star Av. SN2 43 G1
Northampton St. SN1 44 B1

Northbrook Rd. SN2 39 G5
Northern Rd. SN2 39 G6
Northfield Way. SN3 45 E1
Northleaze Clo. SN2 39 F4
Norton Gro. SN3 44 B2
Norwood Clo. SN3 45 F4
Nuffield Clo. SN5 42 C1
Nuthatch Clo. SN3 45 G2
Nutmeg Clo. SN2 38 D3
Nyland Rd. SN3 45 E1
Nythe Rd. SN3 41 E5

Oak Garden. SN3 40 D3
Oak Tree Av. SN2 40 A4
Oakford Walk. SN3 44 D2
Oakham Clo. SN5 42 C3
Oaksey Rd. SN2 39 H2
Oakwood Rd. SN5 42 C1
Oasthouse Clo. SN5 38 A6
Ocotol Way. SN1 44 B1
Odstock Rd. SN2 39 H1
Okebourne Pk. SN3 45 F5
Okeford Clo. SN3 45 E1
Okus Gro. SN2 40 B3
Okus Rd. SN1 43 F4
Old Mill La. SN3 44 B4
Old Shaw La. SN5 42 B1
Olive Gro. SN2 39 G4
Oliver Clo. SN5 42 A2
Omdurman St. SN2 39 H6
Orchard Gro. SN2 40 B3
Orchid Clo. SN2 39 H3
Oriel St. SN1 43 H2
Orkney Clo. SN5 42 B2
Orlando Clo. SN5 42 A3
Orrin Clo. SN5 38 C5
Orwell Clo. SN2 39 F2
Osborne St. SN2 39 G6
Osprey Clo. SN3 45 G2
Osterley Rd. SN2 39 E1
Overbrooke. SN3 45 E4
Overton Gdns. SN3 41 E5
Owl Clo. SN3 45 G2
Oxford Rd. SN3 40 D5
Oxford St. SN1 43 G2

Packington Clo. SN5 42 B1
Paddington Dri. SN5 43 E2
Paddock Clo. SN2 39 E2
Pakenham Rd. SN3 45 E4
Parham Walk. SN5 42 A3
Park La. SN1 43 F2
Park Side. SN3 40 D4
Park Springs. SN5 42 D3
Park St. SN3 41 E5
Parklands Rd. SN3 44 B3
Parr Clo. SN5 42 A2
Parsley Clo. SN2 38 D2
Parsonage Rd. SN3 40 D3
Partridge Clo. SN5 45 H2
Passmore Clo. SN3 45 G1
Pasture Clo. SN2 43 E1
Patney Walk. SN3 39 G1
Paulet Clo. SN5 42 A3
Peaks Down. SN5 38 B4
Pearce Clo. SN2 40 C1
Pearl Rd. SN5 42 A1
Peatmoor Way. SN5 38 B5
Pembroke Gdns. SN2 39 E4
Pembroke St. SN1 43 G3
Pen Clo. SN2 39 G3
Pencarrow. SN2 39 E1
Pendennis Rd. SN5 42 B4
Penfold Gdns. SN1 43 H4
Penhill Dri. SN2 39 H1
Penny La. SN3 44 C1
Pennycress Clo. SN2 39 E2
Pentridge Clo. SN3 45 F1
Penzance Dri. SN5 43 E3
Pepperbox Hill. SN5 38 B5
Percheron Clo. SN5 42 B1
Percy St. SN2 43 F3
Peregrine Clo. SN3 41 F6
Periwinkle Clo. SN2 38 C3
Petersfield Rd. SN3 45 E4
Pevensey Way. SN5 42 C3
Pewsham Rd. SN2 40 A2
Pheasant Clo. SN3 45 G2
Pickwick Clo. SN2 40 B2
Picton Rd. SN5 42 B1
Pigeon House La. SN3 40 D4
Pilgrim Clo. SN5 42 C3
Pilton Clo. SN5 42 B1
Pinehurst Rd. SN2 39 G5
Pinetree Rise. SN2 39 G4
Pinnegar Way. SN3 45 G2
Pinnocks Pl. SN2 40 C3
Pioneer Clo. SN5 42 A1

Pipers Way. SN3 44 A6
Pipitdene. SN3 45 G1
Plattes Clo. SN5 38 C6
Pleydell Rd. SN1 44 A5
Plymouth St. SN1 44 A2
Poltondale. SN5 45 G1
Pond St. SN2 39 E2
Ponting St. SN1 44 A1
Poole Rd. SN2 39 E3
Pope Clo. SN2 39 E1
Poplar Av. SN2 39 H4
Popplechurch Dri. SN3 45 G1
Portal Rd. SN2 39 G5
Portland Av. SN1 43 G4
Portmore Clo. SN5 38 C5
Portsmouth St. SN1 44 B2
Potterdown Rd. SN2 39 H1
Poulton St. SN2 39 H6
Pound La. SN2 39 E2
Poynings Way. SN5 42 A3
Primrose Clo. SN2 38 D2
Princes St. SN1 44 A2
Priory Rd. SN3 44 D4
Pritchard Clo. SN2 40 C2
Prospect Hill. SN1 44 A3
Prospect Pl. SN1 44 A3
Purbeck Clo. SN3 45 E1
Purley Av. SN3 45 E5
Purslane Clo. SN3 38 C3
Purton Rd. SN2 38 D3

Quarry Brook Clo. SN3 41 G2
Quarry Mews. SN1 43 H4
Quarry Rd. SN1 43 H4
Queen St. SN1 43 G2
Queenborough. SN5 42 C4
Queens Dri. SN3 44 B2
Queensfield. SN2 40 B1
Quentin Rd. SN3 44 B4

Radcot Clo. SN5 38 B6
Radley Clo. SN3 45 E1
Radnor St. SN1 43 G3
Radstock Av. SN3 45 E2
Radway Rd. SN3 40 D4
Raglan Clo. SN3 44 C5
Rainer Clo. SN3 41 E4
Raleigh Av. SN3 44 C2
Ramleaze Dri. SN5 42 B1
Ramsbury Av. SN2 39 G1
Ramsden Rd. SN5 42 A5
Ramsthorne Clo. SN2 38 D3
Randall Cres. SN5 42 B1
Randolph Clo. SN3 44 C2
Rannoch Clo. SN5 38 C5
Ransome Rd. SN5 38 B6
Ratcombe Rd. SN5 38 B4
Ravenglass Rd. SN5 42 C2
Ravenscroft. SN3 45 F1
Rawlings Clo. SN3 41 G3
Rawston Clo. SN5 45 F2
Ray Clo. SN2 39 F2
Raybrook Cres. SN3 43 E2
Rayfield Gro. SN2 39 G6
Read St. SN1 43 G3
Reading St. SN1 43 G2
Redcap Gdns. SN5 42 B1
Redcliffe St. SN2 43 F3
Redlynch Clo. SN2 39 H1
Redruth Clo. SN3 45 E3
Regent St. SN1 43 H2
Regents Pl. SN1 44 C6
Retingham Way. SN3 40 D2
Revell Clo. SN2 40 B2
Rhuddlan. SN5 42 C4
Richmond Rd. SN3 39 F6
Ridge Grn. SN5 42 C1
Ridge Nether Moor.
  SN3 45 G5
Ridgeway Clo. SN3 39 E4
Ridgeway Rd. SN2 40 B1
Ringwood Clo. SN3 45 E2
Rinsdale Clo. SN5 38 C5
Ripley Rd. SN1 44 A4
Ripon Way. SN3 45 E1
Ripplefield. SN5 42 B4
Risingham Mead. SN5 42 C3
Rivenhall Rd. SN5 42 C2
Riverdale Clo. SN3 44 A6
Rivermead Dri. SN5 42 C1
Robins Grn. SN3 45 F1
Robinson Clo. SN3 45 F2
Roche Clo. SN3 45 F4
Rochester Clo. SN5 42 B4
Rochford Clo. SN5 42 A3
Rockdown Ct. SN3 39 H2
Rodbourne Grn. SN2 39 F5
Rodbourne Rd. SN2 39 F6

Rodwell Clo. SN3 44 D3
Rogers Clo. SN3 44 D1
Roman Cres. SN1 43 G5
Romney Way. SN5 42 B2
Romsey St. SN2 43 F1
Rose Dale Rd. SN3 44 D4
Rose St. SN2 43 E1
Rosebery St. SN1 44 A1
Rosemary Clo. SN2 38 D2
Ross Gdns. SN3 40 D2
Rother Clo. SN2 39 E2
Roughmoor Way. SN5 42 B1
Roundway Down. SN5 42 C5
Rowan Rd. SN2 39 F4
Rowland Hill Clo. SN3 45 G4
Rowton Heath Way.
  SN5 42 B3
Royston Rd. SN3 44 D4
Ruckley Gdns. SN3 41 E5
Rushall Clo. SN2 39 G2
Rushton Rd. SN3 44 D4
Ruskin Av. SN2 40 C3
Russell Walk. SN3 44 C2
Russley Clo. SN5 38 A5
Ryan Clo. SN5 38 C4
Rycote Clo. SN5 42 B2
Rydal Clo. SN2 39 F2
Rye Clo. SN5 42 B1

Sackville Clo. SN3 44 C1
Saddleback Rd. SN5 42 B1
Sadler Walk. SN3 44 C3
Saffron Clo. SN2 38 D3
Sage Clo. SN2 38 D2
St Albans Clo. SN2 43 E1
St Ambrose Clo. SN3 45 G2
St Andrews Grn. SN3 45 G1
St Helens Vw. SN1 43 F4
St James Clo. SN2 40 B2
St Katherines Grn. SN3 45 G1
St Margarets Rd. SN3 44 A4
St Marys Gro. SN3 39 G6
St Pauls Dri. SN3 45 F1
St Pauls St. SN2 39 H6
St Philips Rd. SN2 40 B3
Salcombe Gro. SN3 44 C3
Salisbury St. SN1 44 A1
Saltram Clo. SN3 45 E2
Sandacre Rd. SN5 38 A6
*Sandford Ct,
  Springfield Rd. SN1 44 A4
Sandgate. SN3 41 E5
Sandown Av. SN3 44 B4
Sandpiper Bri. SN3 45 G1
Sandringham Rd. SN3 44 C4
Sandwood Clo. SN5 38 C5
Sandy La. SN1 43 G4
Sanford St. SN1 43 H2
Sarsen Clo. SN1 43 F4
Savernake St. SN1 43 H3
Scarborough Rd. SN2 39 F6
School Row. SN2 39 E3
Scotby Av. SN3 44 B5
*Scotney Cres,
  Bicton Rd. SN3 39 F1
Seaton Clo. SN3 39 F2
Sedgebrook. SN3 45 F5
Selby Cres. SN5 42 B3
Severn Av. SN2 39 F2
Seymour Rd. SN3 44 C2
Shaftesbury Av. SN3 45 E5
Shakespeare Path. SN2 40 C3
Shalbourne Clo. SN2 39 G2
Shanklin Rd. SN2 39 E3
Shaplands. SN3 40 D4
Shapwick Clo. SN3 45 F1
Sharp Clo. SN5 42 C1
Shaw Rd. SN5 42 C1
Sheen Clo. SN5 42 A4
Shelfinch. SN3 45 G4
Shelley St. SN1 43 G4
Shenton Clo. SN3 41 E4
Sheppard St. SN1 43 G2
Shepperton Way. SN2 39 F1
Sherbourne Pl. SN3 45 E1
Sherford Rd. SN3 39 E3
Sherston Av. SN2 39 H2
Sherwood Clo. SN3 41 E3
Sherwood Rd. SN3 45 E4
Shetland Clo. SN5 42 B1
Shipton Gro. SN3 44 B3
Shire Clo. SN5 42 B1
Shire Ct. SN5 43 F3
Shirley Clo. SN5 44 C1
Shrewsbury Rd. SN3 44 C2
Shrewton Walk. SN3 39 H1
Shrivenham Rd. SN1 44 B1
Shropshire Clo. SN5 42 B1

Sidney Clo. SN5 42 A3
Signal Way. SN3 44 B4
Silchester Way. SN5 42 C2
Silto Ct. SN2 39 F5
Silverton Rd. SN3 45 E2
Simnel Clo. SN5 42 A3
Slade Dri. SN3 40 D6
Sleaford Clo. SN5 42 A2
Smitan Brook. SN3 45 F2
Snowdrop Clo. SN2 38 D2
Snowshill Clo. SN2 39 F2
Somerdale Clo. SN5 42 C2
Somerford Clo. SN2 40 A3
Somerset Rd. SN2 39 F5
Somerville Rd. SN3 44 C2
Sound Copse. SN5 38 B4
South St. SN1 44 A3
South View Av. SN3 44 B2
Southampton St. SN1 44 B2
Southbrook St. SN2 39 G6
Southernwood Dri. SN2 38 C2
Southwick Av. SN3 39 G2
Sparcells Dri. SN5 38 C4
Speedwell Clo. SN2 39 E1
Spencer Clo. SN5 42 A1
Spencer Clo. SN3 44 D1
Spereshott. SN5 42 D4
Spring Gdns. SN1 44 A2
Spring Hill Clo. SN5 42 C3
Springfield Rd. SN1 44 A4
Spur Way. SN2 40 C3
Squires Copse. SN5 38 B5
Stafford St. SN1 43 G3
Stamford Clo. SN5 42 C3
Stanbridge Pk. SN5 42 B1
Stancombe Pk. SN5 42 D3
Standings Clo. SN5 38 A6
Stanier St. SN1 43 H3
Stanley St. SN1 44 A3
Stanmore St. SN1 43 G3
Stansfield Clo. SN5 42 D4
Stanway Clo. SN3 44 D3
Stapleford Clo. SN3 39 G1
Staring Clo. SN5 38 A6
Station App. SN1 44 A4
Station Rd. SN1 43 H1
Stenness Clo. SN5 38 C4
Stephens Rd. SN3 40 D6
Stewart Clo. SN3 39 G1
Stirling Rd. SN3 41 F1
*Stockbridge Copse,
  Ratcombe Rd. SN5 38 B4
Stockton Rd. SN2 39 H2
Stokesay Dri. SN5 42 C3
Stone La. SN5 38 A5
Stonecrop Way. SN2 39 E1
Stonefield Clo. SN5 42 C1
Stonehill Grn. SN5 42 D2
Stonehurst Rd. SN3 40 D6
Stoneybeck Clo. SN5 38 B4
Stour Rd. SN5 42 B3
Stratford Clo. SN5 42 D3
Stratton Orchard. SN3 40 D4
Stratton Rd. SN1 40 C6
Stratton St Margaret
  By-Pass. SN3 40 B1
Stuart Clo. SN3 44 D2
Stubsmead. SN3 45 F3
Studland Clo. SN3 45 E4
Sudeley Way. SN5 42 B3
Suffolk St. SN2 39 H6
Summers St. SN2 43 F1
Sunningdale Rd. SN3 39 H3
Sunnyside Av. SN1 43 F3
Surrey Rd. SN2 39 F5
Sutton Rd. SN3 45 F4
Swallowdale. SN3 45 F1
Swallowfield Av. SN3 44 C3
Swanage Walk. SN3 39 E3
Swanbrook. SN3 41 F6
Swindon Rd. SN3 40 D6
Swindon Rd. SN1 44 A3
Swinley Dri. SN5 38 A5
Sycamore Gro. SN2 39 H4
Symonds. SN3 42 B5
Syon Clo. SN2 39 F1
Sywell Rd. SN3 41 F6

Tamar Clo. SN3 39 G3
Tamworth Dri. SN5 42 B2
Tansley Moor. SN3 45 G5
Tarragon Clo. SN2 38 C3
Tattershall. SN5 42 C4
Taunton St. SN1 43 G2
Tavistock Rd. SN3 45 E4
Tawny Owl Clo. SN3 41 E6
Taylor Cres. SN3 40 D2
Tealsbrook. SN3 45 G1

Tedder Clo. SN2 3
Tees Clo. SN2 3
Teeswater Clo. SN5 4
Telford Way. SN5 4
Temple St. SN1 4
Tennyson St. SN1 4
Tensing Gdns. SN2 3
Terncliff. SN3 4
Tewkesbury Way. SN5 4
Thackeray Clo. SN3 4
Thames Av. SN2 3
The Acorns. SN3 44
The Birches. SN3 44
The Bramptons. SN5 42
The Brow. SN2 3
The Bungalows. SN3 39
The Buntings. SN3 4
The Chesters. SN5 42
The Circle. SN2 39
The Close. SN3 4
The Crescent. SN5 38
The Drive. SN3 45
The Ferns. SN3 39
The Forum. SN5 42
The Harriers. SN3 45
The Heights. SN1 43
The Holbein. SN5 42
The Knoll. SN1 44
The Mall. SN1 43
The Orchards. SN3 44
The Owletts. SN3 45
The Paddocks. SN3 40
The Parade. SN1 43
The Planks. SN3 43
The Quarries. SN1 43
The Square. SN1 44
The Street. SN2 39
The Weavers. SN3 44
The Willows. SN5 38
Thirlmere. SN3 45
Thomas St. SN2 43
Thornbridge Av. SN3 44
Thorne Rd. SN3 45
Thornford Dri. SN5 42
Thornhill Rd. SN3 41 C
Threshel Clo. SN3 39
Thurlestone Rd. SN3 44
Thurney Dri. SN5 42
Thyme Clo. SN3 38
Tilleys La. SN3 40
Tilshead Walk. SN3 39 H
Timandra Clo. SN2 39 F
Tintagel Clo. SN5 42 C
Tisbury Clo. SN3 39 H
Tismeads Cres. SN1 44 A
Titchfield Clo. SN5 42 A
Tithe Barn Cres. SN1 43 F
Tiverton Rd. SN2 39 H
Tockenham Way. SN2 39 F
Tollard Clo. SN3 45 F
Torridge Clo. SN2 39 E
Totterdown Clo. SN3 45 G
Tovey Rd. SN2 39 G
Towcester Rd. SN3 41 E
Tower Rd. SN5 38 B
Tracy Clo. SN2 39 F
Trajan Rd. SN3 41 F
Tree Courts Rd. SN2 39 G
Tregantle Walk. SN5 42 E
Tregoze Way. SN5 42 A
Trent Rd. SN2 39 F
Trentham Clo. SN3 44 D
Trinity Clo. SN3 44 D
Trueman Clo. SN3 45 F
Truro Path. SN5 42 C
Tryon Clo. SN3 45 G
Tudor Cres. SN3 41 E5
Tulip Tree Clo. SN3 39 H
Turl St. SN1 43 H2
Turner St. SN1 43 F3
Turnham Grn. SN5 42 B4
Tweed Clo. SN2 39 E2
Twyford Clo. SN3 44 D1
Tyburn Clo. SN5 42 B2
Tydeman St. SN2 40 A5
Tye Gdns. SN5 42 A3
Tyndale Path. SN5 42 A2
Tyneham Rd. SN2 45 E2

Ullswater Clo. SN3 45 G4
Union St. SN1 44 A3
Upfield. SN3 45 G4
Upham Rd. SN3 44 B3
Uxbridge Rd. SN5 42 A4

Valleyside. SN1 43 F4

TISBURY

TROWBRIDGE

Oriel Clo. BA14 47 G2
Osborne Rd. BA14 47 F3
Painters Mead. BA14 47 G4
Palmer Rd. BA14 47 E4
Park Rd. BA14 47 E6
Park St. BA14 48 D1
Parklands. BA14 46 D3
Paxcroft Way. BA14 47 F6
Pembroke Clo. BA14 48 E2
Pepperacre La. BA14 47 F4
Pitman Av. BA14 48 C2
Pitman Ct. BA14 48 C2
Polebarn Rd. BA14 47 E5
Pound Farm Clo. BA14 47 F2
Princess Gdns. BA14 47 F1
Prospect Pl. BA14 47 E4
Quarterway La. BA14 47 F5
Queens Club Gdns.
   BA14 46 B6
Queens Gdns. BA14 47 F1
Queens Rd. BA14 46 D4
Quilling Clo. BA14 47 F4
Ragleth Gro. BA14 47 F4
Raleigh Ct. BA14 47 E5
Rambler Clo. BA14 46 B5
Ramsbury Walk. BA14 48 E3
Ravenscroft Gdns.
   BA14 47 F5
Red Hat La. BA14 46 D5
Richmond Clo. BA14 48 B1
River Way. BA14 46 C5
Rock Rd. BA14 48 C2
Rodsleigh. BA14 48 A2
Rodwell Pk. BA14 47 F4
Rosedale Gdns. BA14 46 A5
Rossett Gdns. BA14 46 B6
Roundstone St. BA14 47 E5
Rutland Cres. BA14 48 D2
St Augustines Rd. BA14 46 C6
St Johns Cres. BA14 48 A3
St Margarets Clo. BA14 48 B3
St Marys Clo. BA14 47 F1
St Marys Gdns. BA14 47 F2
St Michaels Clo. BA14 47 G3
St Stephens Pl. BA14 47 E6
St Thomas Pass. BA14 47 E5
St Thomas Rd. BA14 47 E5
Sanders Rd. BA14 46 D4
Sandown Centre. BA14 48 F4
Sandringham Rd. BA14 48 C3
Saxon Dri. BA14 47 E1
Seymour Ct. BA14 46 D5
Seymour Rd. BA14 46 D4
Shaftesbury Ct. BA14 48 B2
Shails La. BA14 46 D5
Shearman St. BA14 48 E2
Sheepcote Barton. BA14 48 F1
Sherborne Rd. BA14 46 A5
Shore Pl. BA14 46 A5
Shrewton Clo. BA14 48 E3
Silver Birch Gro. BA14 48 C3
Silver Mdws. BA14 48 B3
Silver St. BA14 47 E5
Silver St La. BA14 48 B3
Slowgrove Clo. BA14 47 F6
Smithy Well Clo. BA14 47 G5
Sorrell Clo. BA14 48 E3
South View Rd. BA14 48 E3
Southway. BA14 48 E1
Southwood Rd. BA14 47 G6
Speedwell Clo. BA14 48 E1
Spinners Croft. BA14 48 E1
Springfield Clo. BA14 47 F4
Springfield Pk. BA14 47 F4
Stallard St. BA14 46 D6
Stancomb Av. BA14 47 E5
Stanton Clo. BA14 48 E3
Station Way. BA14 46 D5
Stonelea. BA14 47 H3
Stuart Clo. BA14 47 E1
Studley Rise. BA14 48 E2
Summerdown Walk.
   BA14 48 D4
Summerleaze. BA14 48 B2
Surrey Pl. BA14 48 E3
Swallow Clo. BA14 46 B6
Swan Dri. BA14 47 F1
Sycamore Gro. BA14 48 C3
Talbot Rd. BA14 48 B2
Thestfield Dri. BA14 47 F1
The Beeches. BA14 47 G4
The Croft. BA14 48 D2
The Down. BA14 47 E4
The Halve. BA14 47 E5
The Knapp. BA14 47 G3
The Mount. BA14 47 E4
The Poplars. BA14 48 B3
The Slipway. BA14 47 F1

Timbrell St. BA14 47 E5
Tower Clo. BA14 48 B1
Town Bridge. BA14 46 D5
Towpath Rd. BA14 47 E1
Trowbridge Rd. BA14 47 G3
Trowle. BA14 46 A2
Tudor Dri. BA14 47 E1
Tyning Clo. BA14 48 A1
Union St. BA14 47 E5
Upper Broad St. BA14 46 D5
Victoria Gdns. BA14 47 F3
Victoria Rd. BA14 47 F3
Walmesley Chase.
   BA14 47 G5
Walnut Gro. BA14 48 C3
Warbler Clo. BA14 46 B6
Warburton Clo. BA14 48 B2
Waterworks Rd. BA14 48 C1
Weavers Dri. BA14 48 E1
Webbers Ct. BA14 48 A3
Wesley Rd. BA14 48 D1
West Ashton Rd. BA14 47 E6
West St. BA14 48 C1
Westbourne Gdns.
   BA14 46 C6
Westbourne Rd. BA14 48 C1
Westcroft St. BA14 46 D4
Westfield Clo. BA14 48 B2
Westfield Rd. BA14 48 A2
Westmead Cres. BA14 48 A4
Westwood Rd. BA14 46 A5
Whaddon La. BA14 47 H2
White Hart Yard. BA14 47 E5
White Horse Clo. BA14 48 E2
White Row Hill. BA14 48 B4
White Row Pk. BA14 48 B3
Wicker Hill. BA14 46 D5
Widbrook Meadow.
   BA14 46 A6
Wilcot Clo. BA14 48 D3
Willow Gro. BA14 48 C3
Wilton Dri. BA14 48 E2
Wiltshire Dri. BA14 48 D3
Windermere Rd. BA14 47 E4
Windsor Dri. BA14 48 C4
Wingfield Rd. BA14 48 B1
Winterslow Rd. BA14 48 C4
Withy Clo. BA14 47 E2
Woburn La. BA14 46 B5
Woodborough Clo.
   BA14 48 E3
Woodmill Ter. BA14 47 H3
Woodhouse Gdns.
   BA14 47 H4
Woolpack Mdws. BA14 48 F2
Worsted Clo. BA14 48 F1
Wren Clo. BA14 46 C6
Wyke Rd. BA14 47 E2
Yarn Ter. BA14 48 F2
Yeoman Way. BA14 48 D2
Yerbury St. BA14 47 E5
York Buildings. BA14 47 E4

WARMINSTER

Alcock Crest. BA12 50 B4
Arn Vw. BA12 50 C1
Ash Walk. BA12 50 C3
Ashley Coombe. BA12 50 C6
Ashley Pl. BA12 50 C6
Avon Rd. BA12 50 D5
Barley Clo. BA12 51 F5
Bath Rd. BA12 50 B1
Battlesbury Rd. BA12 51 G4
Beacon View. BA12 50 A4
Beavens Ct. BA12 51 E3
Beckfield Clo. BA12 51 E4
Beech Av. BA12 50 C4
Beech Gro. BA12 50 D2
Bell Clo. BA12 50 C5
Bell Hill. BA12 50 C5
Bishopstrow Ct. BA12 51 H5
Bishopstrow Rd. BA12 51 G5
Blackdown Clo. BA12 50 D2
Blenheim Clo. BA12 50 C3
Boot Hill. BA12 50 C5
Bore Hill. BA12 50 C6
Boreham Clo. BA12 51 E4
Boreham Field. BA12 51 G4
Boreham Rd. BA12 51 E4
Bourbon Clo. BA12 50 D5
Bourne Clo. BA12 50 D5
Bradfield Clo. BA12 51 F5
Bradley Clo. BA12 50 B6
Bradley Rd. BA12 50 B6

Bramley Clo. BA12 50 C3
Bread St. BA12 50 C5
Broadway. BA12 50 B5
Broadwood Clo. BA12 50 C4
Brook St. BA12 50 B5
Broxburn Rd. BA12 50 A4
Buttons Yard. BA12 51 E4
Camelia Dri. BA12 50 B3
Cannimore Clo. BA12 50 B5
Cannimore Rd. BA12 50 A6
Canons Clo. BA12 50 E5
Chain La. BA12 51 E4
Chalfield Clo. BA12 50 C1
Chancery La. BA12 51 E4
Chantry Mews. BA12 50 A3
Chapel St. BA12 50 C5
*Chathat Ct,
   Yard Ct. BA12 51 E3
Chelwood Ct. BA12 51 E4
Chiltern Clo. BA12 50 D2
Christchurch Ter. BA12 50 A4
Church St. BA12 50 C3
Cley Vw. BA12 50 B4
Cobbett Pl. BA12 50 C4
Cobbett Rise. BA12 51 H6
Coldharbour La. BA12 50 C4
Coleridge Clo. BA12 50 A4
Conference Clo. BA12 50 C4
Copheap La. BA12 51 E2
Copheap Rise. BA12 51 E2
Corner Grd. BA12 51 G5
Cotswold Clo. BA12 50 D2
Cotton House Gdns.
   BA12 51 E3
Cuckoos Nest La. BA12 50 B4
Damask Way. BA12 50 D5
Daniell Crest. BA12 50 C4
Deverill Rd. BA12 50 C6
Dorothy Walk. BA12 50 C2
Downs Vw. BA12 51 F4
East End Av. BA12 50 D4
East St. BA12 51 E4
Ebble Cres. BA12 50 C5
Elm Hill. BA12 51 E2
Emwell St. BA12 50 C3
Epping Clo. BA12 50 D2
Factory La. BA12 50 C4
Fairfield Rd. BA12 51 E3
Fanshaw Way. BA12 50 D5
Ferris Mead. BA12 50 D4
Firbank Cres. BA12 51 F2
Flers Ct. BA12 50 C3
Folly La. BA12 50 A5
Fore St. BA12 50 C2
Foxley Clo. BA12 50 C2
Freesia Clo. BA12 50 B3
Furlong. BA12 51 E4
Furnax La. BA12 50 C2
George St. BA12 50 D3
George St Pl. BA12 50 D3
Gipsy La. BA12 51 E4
Glebe Field. BA12 50 D4
Goodwin Clo. BA12 51 G2
Grange La. BA12 51 G5
Grenadier Clo. BA12 50 C4
Grovelands Way. BA12 50 B3
Hampton La. BA12 50 C5
Heathlands. BA12 50 B5
Henfords Marsh. BA12 51 E6
Heron Slade. BA12 51 F5
High St. BA12 50 D3
Highbury Pk. BA12 51 E4
Hillbourne Clo. BA12 50 D3
Hillwood Clo. BA12 50 C5
Hillwood La. BA12 50 C5
Hollybush Rd. BA12 50 D3
Houldsworth Av. BA12 51 G2
Imber Rd. BA12 51 E3
Imber Way. BA12 51 F3
Imberwood Clo. BA12 51 E3
INDUSTRIAL ESTATES:
Crusader Park
   Business Pk. BA12 50 B2
Woodcock Ind Est.
   BA12 51 F3
Kennet Clo. BA12 50 C5
King Ct. BA12 50 B5
King La. BA12 50 B5
King St. BA12 50 B5
Kings Rise. BA12 50 B5
Langholme Av. BA12 50 A4
Langholme Clo. BA12 50 A4
Little Orchard. BA12 50 C4
Lower Marsh Rd. BA12 50 D5
Ludlow Clo. BA12 50 D5
Luxfield Rd. BA12 50 B3
Lyme Av. BA12 50 C4
Maddocks Hill. BA12 50 B5

Malvern Clo. BA12 50 D2
Manor Gdns. BA12 50 C3
Market Pl. BA12 50 D3
Marsh St. BA12 50 C5
Martin Crest. BA12 50 B5
Masefield Rd. BA12 50 A4
Melrose Av. BA12 50 B4
Melrose Clo. BA12 50 B4
Mendip Clo. BA12 50 D2
Middleton Clo. BA12 50 D2
Minster Vw. BA12 50 B3
Morley Fields. BA12 51 E3
Mount La. BA12 50 C5
Myrtle Av. BA12 50 C4
Newopaul Way. BA12 50 C1
Newport. BA12 50 D3
Norridge Vw. BA12 50 B3
North La. BA12 50 A3
North Row. BA12 50 D3
Orchard Clo. BA12 51 E2
Pampas Ct. BA12 50 A4
Pepper Pl. BA12 51 F3
Perriwinkle Clo. BA12 50 A4
Pit Mead La. BA12 51 H6
Plants Grn. BA12 51 E4
Portway. BA12 50 D3
Portway La. BA12 50 C2
Poulsden La. BA12 50 D5
Pound Row. BA12 50 B4
Pound St. BA12 50 B4
Prestbury Dri. BA12 51 E5
Primrose Wk. BA12 50 C2
Princecroft La. BA12 50 C4
Quantock Clo. BA12 50 D2
Queensway. BA12 51 G4
Rectory Clo. BA12 50 C2
Regal Ct. BA12 50 D4
Robin Clo. BA12 51 E4
Rock La. BA12 51 F4
Ruskin Dri. BA12 50 A4
Russett Ct. BA12 50 C3
Sack Hill. BA12 51 H1
St Andrews Rd. BA12 50 A5
St Georges Clo. BA12 51 G5
St Johns Rd. BA12 51 E5
Sambourne Chase.
   BA12 50 C3
Sambourne Gdns. BA12 50 C4
Sambourne Rd. BA12 50 C4
Sassoon Clo. BA12 50 A4
Savernake Clo. BA12 50 D2
Saxons Acre. BA12 50 C4
Shelley Way. BA12 50 A4
Sherwood Clo. BA12 50 C2
Silver St. BA12 50 C3
Smallbrook La. BA12 51 F5
Smallbrook Rd. BA12 51 E4
South St. BA12 50 B4
Southleigh Vw. BA12 51 B5
Station Rd. BA12 50 D3
Stephens Way. BA12 50 C2
Stuart Grn. BA12 50 D4
Swallow Clo. BA12 50 B5
Swift Mead. BA12 50 B5
Teichman Clo. BA12 51 E4
Tennyson Clo. BA12 50 A4
Thames Clo. BA12 50 D5
The Avenue. BA12 50 D3
The Close. BA12 50 D3
The Dene. BA12 51 G4
The Downlands. BA12 51 E3
The Grove. BA12 50 A4
The Homelands. BA12 50 B5
The Maltings. BA12 50 C4
The Mead. BA12 50 D2
The Oaks. BA12 50 D2
The Paddock. BA12 51 E4
The Pippins. BA12 50 C3
The Ridgeway. BA12 50 D4
The Teasels. BA12 50 C4
The Uplands. BA12 51 E3
Thornhill Rd. BA12 50 A5
Upper Marsh Rd. BA12 50 D4
Upton Clo. BA12 50 B4
Vicarage St. BA12 50 C3
Victoria Mews. BA12 50 C3
Victoria Rd. BA12 50 C3
Virginia Dri. BA12 50 B3
Watery La. BA12 51 H6
Were Clo. BA12 50 B3
West Leigh. BA12 50 B4
West Parade. BA12 50 C4
West St. BA12 50 C4
West St Pl. BA12 50 B4
Westbury Rd. BA12 50 D4
Weymouth St. BA12 50 D4
Whitfield Clo. BA12 51 E3
Willow Cres. BA12 51 E5

Wilson Sq. BA12
Woodcock Gdns. BA12
Woodcock La. BA12
Woodcock Rd. BA12
Woodland Rd. BA12
Woodman Mead. BA12
Wren Clo. BA12
Wylye Clo. BA12
Wylye Rd. BA12
Yard Ct. BA12

WESTBURY

Abbotts Ct. BA13 52
Alfred St. BA13 52
Anne Clo. BA13 52
Arundell Clo. BA13 52
Ash Gro. BA13 52
Audley Gate. BA13 52
Avebury Clo. BA13 52
Beech Gro. BA13 52
Bell Orchard. BA13 52
Bitham La. BA13 52
Bitham Pk. BA13 52
Blackhorse La. BA13 52
Bratton Rd. BA13 52
Bremeridge Rd. BA13 52
Briar Clo. BA13 52
Brook La. BA13 52
Brunel Clo. BA13 52
Castle Vw. BA13 52
Cedar Gro. BA13 52
Chalford Gdns. BA13 52
Chantry La. BA13 52
Chestnut Gro. BA13 52
Cheyney Walk. BA13 52
Chichester Pk. BA13 52
Church La. BA13 52
Church St. BA13 52
Coach Rd. BA13 52
Danvers Way. BA13 52
Dene Clo. BA13 52
Devon Dri. BA13 52
Dog Kennel La. BA13 52
Dorney Clo. BA13 52
Dorset Dri. BA13 52
Downsview Rd. BA13 52
Eden Vale Rd. BA13 52
Edward St. BA13 52
Elm Gro. BA13 52
Fairdown Av. BA13 52
Farleigh Gro. BA13 52
Field Clo. BA13 52
Fore St. BA13 52
Fountain Ct. BA13 52
Frogmore Rd. BA13 52
Gibbs Clo. BA13 52
Gloucester Walk. BA13 52
Grassy Slope. BA13 52
Great Roc Rd. BA13 52 A
Green La. BA13 52 B
Gryphon Clo. BA13 52 A
Ham Rd. BA13 52 A
Hampshire Gdns. BA13 52 A
Hampton Mews. BA13 52
Hawkeridge Pk. BA13 52 A
Hawkeridge Rd. BA13 52
Hawthorn Gro. BA13 52
Haynes Rd. BA13 52 C
Hayward Pl. BA13 52 B
Hazel Gro. BA13 52 B
Heather Clo. BA13 52 B
High St. BA13 52 C
Hillside Pk. BA13 52 D
Hospital Rd. BA13 52 C
Indigo Gdns. BA13 52 B
INDUSTRIAL ESTATES:
Brook Lane
   Ind Est. BA13 52 A2
Woodland
   Ind Est. BA13 52 B2
Ingram Clo. BA13 52 B2
Jubilee Clo. BA13 52 C3
Kendrick Clo. BA13 52 C4
Kingfisher Dri. BA13 52 C2
Lanhams Clo. BA13 52 C4
Laverton Ct. BA13 52 C3
Laverton Grn. BA13 52 B6
Laverton Rd. BA13 52 B5
Leigh Clo. BA13 52 A6
Leigh Rd. BA13 52 B5
Leighton Grn. BA13 52 C5
Leighton La. BA13 52 C5
Leighton Park N. BA13 52 B6
Leighton Park Rd. BA13 52 B6
Leighton Park W. BA13 52 C